PUFFIN BOOKS
A BRUSH WITH INDIAN ART

Mamta Nainy is a children's writer and editor. So she divides her time between writing and editing for children, making doodles that only she finds funny and eating cupcakes. She loves travelling but is too lazy to do it, so she makes do with reading. She spent some years in advertising before an apple fell on her head while she was sitting under a mango tree and she had her eureka moment—she has written some eight books for children since then. Currently she works as consulting senior editor with Katha.

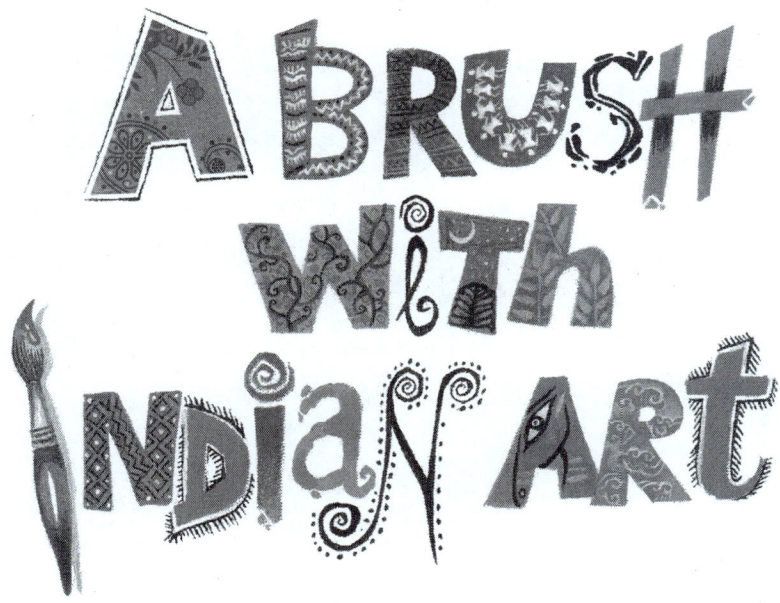

A BRUSH WITH INDIAN ART

From cave to contemporary paintings

Mamta Nainy

Illustrations by Aniruddha Mukherjee

PUFFIN BOOKS

An imprint of Penguin Random House

PUFFIN BOOKS

USA | Canada | UK | Ireland | Australia
New Zealand | India | South Africa | China | Singapore

Puffin Books is part of the Penguin Random House group of companies
whose addresses can be found at global.penguinrandomhouse.com

Published by Penguin Random House India Pvt. Ltd
4th Floor, Capital Tower 1, MG Road,
Gurugram 122 002, Haryana, India

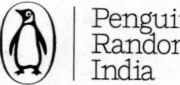

Penguin
Random House
India

First published in Puffin Books by Penguin Random House India 2018

Text copyright © Mamta Nainy 2018
Illustrations copyright © Aniruddha Mukherjee 2018

ISBN 9780143441564

Typeset in Bembo Infant MT Std by Manipal Digital Systems, Manipal
Printed at Replika Press Pvt. Ltd, India

www.penguin.co.in

This is a legitimate digitally printed version of the book and therefore might not
have certain extra finishing on the cover.

For Ona, the wind beneath my wings

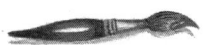

Contents

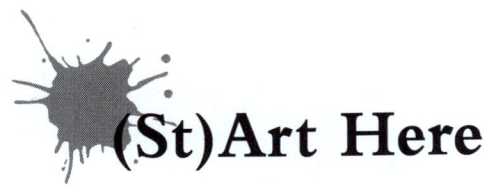 **(St)Art Here**

What can be more fun than the splashes and smears and daubs and blobs of paint on paper, right? But have you ever wondered how exactly art came to be? Who were the first people to paint, and how did art evolve over time? And what *is* art, really? Is it paint splattered on canvas? Or carved pillars in ancient buildings? Or those silly doodles that you make in your notebooks?

Different people have different ideas about art and understand art differently. Some believe that art should be beautiful and show skill, while others believe that art should make people think. Some others say that art is what you see in galleries, while there are those that claim it's all around us. For some, art is the final product created by an artist, while others consider the whole process of creating an artwork—right from finding inspiration and thinking up an idea to the last brushstroke or the final tap of the chisel—to be art.

And guess what? ALL these different notions and conceptions are right! Because art is no *one* thing. It is many, many things: it can be pretty or ugly; it can be happy or sad; it can be quirky or even shocking. It can be on a piece of paper, a wall, a ceiling, a rug . . . anything that you can think of. It can be monochrome, it can be colourful, or even colourfully colourless (if you get the gist!).

For art is ever evolving, and artists across time have always looked at fresh ways of portraying the world around them.

The world is a treasure trove of art of all shapes, styles, sizes and vibes. And its history is sprinkled with shining examples of art and architecture that are held in high regard by people the world over. These works are important not just because they are masterful and simply stunning, but because they hold within themselves stories—stories that mirror our past, present and future. And these stories are sometimes mysterious and sometimes simply fascinating.

This book is about these stories, which have been plucked from the many art traditions in India. It is your ticket to the adventure called Indian art. All you need to do on this journey is add a bit of your imagination and keep your eyes and minds wide open. Sounds exciting? Fun, even? Right, then!

But wait—just some friendly advice before you're on your way!

You can dive into this book anywhere you like—you don't need to begin at the beginning. Of course, if you do read the book from cover to cover, it will be a good way to see how Indian art evolved over time. But you can jump into any chapter or section that rouses your curiosity. In fact, why don't you try reading this book from back to front?

But DON'T try to read the entire book in one sitting. Take your time to enjoy the diverse, wonderful world of Indian art. As you read on, you are even free to add to this repository. Oh, and remember to keep your art supplies handy. Who knows, you might just feel like creating your own masterpieces once you're done reading!

The Big Picture of Indian Art

Indian art has evolved over centuries. Down the years, it has undergone tremendous change because of various factors, such as geography, culture, tradition, religion and politics. And, therefore, it is a patchwork of different forms, styles and themes. This book takes you on a grand tour into the history of Indian art, halting at many fun stops—the numerous artistic traditions and movements in India, its renowned artists, their unforgettable masterpieces, the trends and events that helped spawn them, the many . . . Hold on, don't conjure up visions of memorizing dusty dates and dustier facts just yet! That's NOT the side of art history we're going to dwell on. This book presents a vibrant history of art by piecing together interesting anecdotes and colourful trivia.

Covering millennia of artistic expression, the book time-travels to the different periods in the history of Indian art—right from the age of cave paintings, all the way to contemporary times (and everything in between)—and tells you *why* and *how*, during each epoch, people chose to express themselves through their art. The stories in the following pages will lead you down the rabbit hole of history and plant you in the thick of the country's most significant movements: you can accompany prehistoric cavemen on a hunt; stroll barefoot with Buddhist monks; hobnob with Mughal emperors;

be a part of India's freedom struggle; and look over the shoulders of modern and contemporary artists as they paint. Capturing how art has always been integrated with life, each chapter in the book will give you an intimate glimpse into Indian art history, which is supported by detailed artwork for you to pore over.

As you read the stories of Indian art in this book, you will find that it becomes easier to 'read' the artwork as well. There's no magic formula needed to appreciate Indian art, or art in general, and there are no right or wrong answers—what matters is how you *feel* when you look at a piece of art and how you respond to it. Ask yourself what the artwork makes *you* feel and why. It's quite possible that even while looking at the same piece of art, what you see and feel are quite different from what your friend sees and feels. And this is absolutely fine. When looking at the works, note the surprises and secrets that linger in the fine details. Being curious and asking questions is the starting point. Only then will you notice that art is often full of clues that artists themselves include to help us figure out why they created their works in the way they did.

So, for each artwork, look for more than you can see in the first instance. Try to envision the story behind the artwork, if there is one—or, better yet, think up your own! If by now you think that looking at art is a lot like detective work, you can't be more right!

I hope what you discover and decode in the next few pages sparks a lifelong interest in art, because once you plunge into this magical bottomless ocean, you're bound to bring back an awesome catch of stories, imagination, inspiration and dreams with each dive.

So, shall we?

Mamta Nainy

The First Drawing

Cave Paintings

Rocky Beginnings

Every story has a beginning. So how did the story of art begin, you ask? Well, no one really knows for certain how, where or when art originated. But maybe, just maybe, it began like stories often do . . .

Once upon a time, long, long ago, when the world was still very young—imagine a time before school every morning, homework every evening and private tuition in between—deep in the dark, mysterious caves lived early humans—our ancestors. They survived as nomadic hunter-gatherers, who lived in caves near streams and rivers and foraged for food every single day. They gathered nuts, fruits and berries from the jungle and hunted animals using tools. These tools were made from stone, bone and wood. Since no metals were used, this time period—roughly two million years ago—is called the Stone Age.

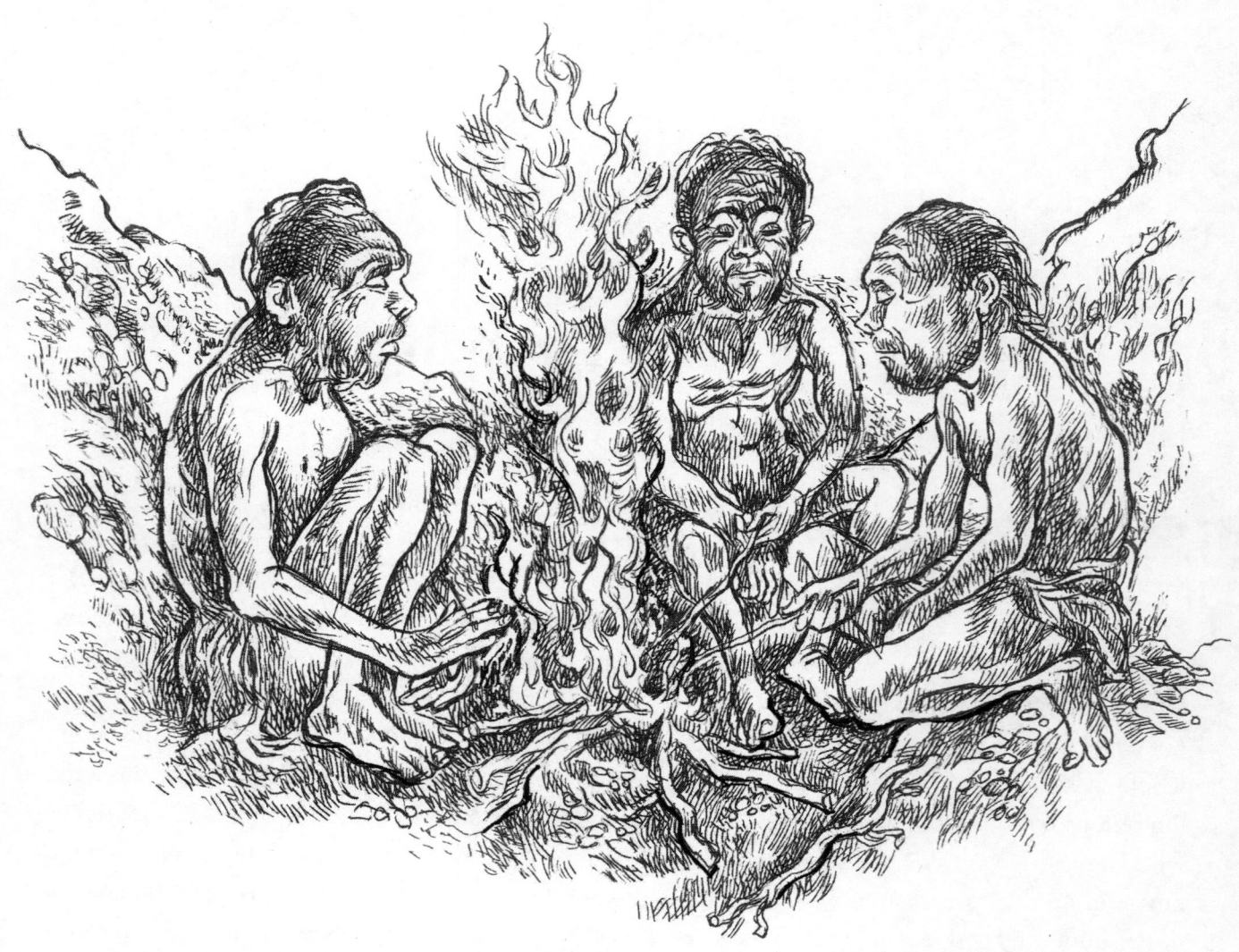

Prehistoric cavemen hanging out around a fire after a long day

Then one day, the early humans struck two stones together—and sparked a fire! This fascinating new discovery allowed them to cook their food, stay warm in the cold, light up their gloomy caves and gather around the crackling fire in small, friendly groups.

Incredibly, after the discovery of fire, our ancestors made another breakthrough. Maybe it happened towards the end of an unusually chilly winter night in a sheltered valley, as the mist hung thick over the grey-brown mountains and three cavemen sat around a fire outside their cave and discussed the day's exploits.

'The cold is getting worse every year,' the first caveman must have said, rubbing his rough hands together. 'I haven't spotted a single herd of horses today, and the elks have all but vanished! I had to wait patiently the whole day before I could find a wild boar a few man-lengths from the cliff. I promptly hefted my spear and, judging the wind's direction, took aim. Look, here it lies before you.' Now, let's imagine he pointed at the carcass that lay in front of him.

'Game is scarce indeed,' the second caveman may have replied, 'but today has been my lucky day. A herd of twenty bison came down to the river soon after the sun had climbed the sky. I crouched low in the damp grass and inched towards them. A few of the beasts sensed danger and started kicking their hooves. But there was this one old bison that dipped its head and charged, its curled horns pointing straight at me! I waited—just when it was a spear-length away, I flung my weapon, which caught the animal right between its shoulder blades. Its front legs buckled and it fell with a thump. And so, here lies my day's booty!' He must have nodded towards the huge bison at his feet.

Let's picture that, at this point, the third caveman first looked at his hunt—a small deer—and then at the other two's. 'I-I couldn't manage a bigger kill . . . I only caught this puny thing at the watering hole,' he may have confessed. 'But if I tell you what I SAW today . . . oh, your hair will stand on end, your spine will tingle, your blood will run cold, your bones will rattle, your—'

'Ha! You always have the big stories, never a big catch!' must have come the reply.

'Fine, don't believe me, but then don't say I didn't warn you,' the third man may have insisted. 'I saw . . . a GIGANTIC FIVE-FOOTED CREATURE today! A kind I've *never* seen before. When it walked, it trampled on a few trees and shook the very earth under its feet!'

'Oh, c'mon!' The other two wouldn't have believed him still. 'Now you will say it was bigger than the elephants or had chompers as sharp as your saw, won't you?'

'Er . . . but it was! It did!'

Eager to show his friends the unusual creature he'd seen, the third caveman must have thought of a plan. He would have scooped dirt from the ground, mixed it with a little water from the river and, using his finger, begun to draw on the wall of the cave. And before he'd have known it, he must have drawn the massive head of the prehistoric wild bear, with small round ears, a short snout and an open mouth showing a row of sharp teeth. Thus the caveman must have brought the fabled beast to life, its image having flowed from his mind, through his fingers, to the wall. It would have seemed like sheer magic, as the creature had 'appeared' through this simple mud-and-water rendition. The caveman must have looked at what he'd just drawn in awe!

'See, *this* is how it looked!' he would have exclaimed as his friends sat spellbound, grunting in appreciation, and then . . . 'Humba! Humba! Bumba! Bumba!' The cavemen must have broken into a celebratory jig!

Maybe this is how art began—or maybe not. What really matters is that art began as a way to express oneself, to make others see what one saw and felt and as a means to tell stories. And to this day, stories continue to be shared through art.

Rewind with Relish

Once early humans discovered drawing and painting, which has now come to be known as cave art, there was no stopping them! They constantly drew. This was their unique method of telling their tales—of their desires, their triumphs and their losses, and their life itself. Just as we do now, our ancestors drew all that they saw around them, and their caves became their canvasses. They painted on the walls, on the roofs, and even in little nooks and crannies and dark, narrow passageways that were hard to access. Why did they draw at spots that were difficult to reach, do you think? What if they wanted to make some corrections later? Well, that's a mystery that no one has solved.

As the cavemen made more discoveries—about the surrounding jungles, about other creatures, about their own selves and their friends—they started sketching these as well. They drew any unusual creatures they encountered and stencilled their hands on the walls of the caves, almost like signatures on their artwork. But most of all, they drew the animals they hunted. Gradually, they started drawing human figures next to the animals. Were they drawing themselves? Was this their way of celebrating a good hunt? Or expressing the unique relationship early humans shared with animals? Or maybe they were just a bored lot—remember, they didn't have TVs or mobile phones—who found art entertaining! Perhaps it was all this and more. Whatever their reasons and motivations, what we do know for sure is that art began in ancient times and that these early paintings remain a beautiful link to a time long ago.

Let's Go Cave-Hunting!

So where are these stunning art-adorned caves, you ask? Well, everywhere! Cave paintings can be found almost all over the world. The first ones were discovered in Europe and are said to be some 35,000 years old.

In the Cave of Altamira in Spain, we can find some of the most amazing cave art created about 14,000 years ago. There are nearly hundreds of animal figures painted on the roof, but the most famous of these are those of the bison. The Altamira cave paintings are done in an extremely modern style for such an ancient time—while most cave paintings in the world are composed of sharp outlines, these drawings are filled with colours of varying intensity that give the impression of depth.

Many other parts of the world too have their share of well-known cave paintings, like Serra da Capivara in Brazil, Magura in Bulgaria, Tadrart Acacus in Libya, Cueva de las Manos in Argentina, Lascaux in France, Kakadu in Australia, and, of course, our very own Bhimbetka in India.

Palette of the Past

In those days, colours didn't come in tubes and bottles. So you must be wondering how the early humans painted, right? Well, they used whatever they could get their hands on. Ancient cavemen

Picture This

You're hiking across wooded hills. Thick trees tower above you and prickly bushes brush against your legs. It's the great outdoors at its best! Then suddenly, you see something—the dense foliage has given way to a small opening. You're curious, of course, so you peek inside but can't see a thing. It's as dark as the inside of a hippopotamus! You scrape through the opening with a torch and lo, a whole treasure trove of prehistoric art greets you!

This is exactly what happened to four teenagers and their pet dog. They had accidentally discovered the Lascaux Caves in France.

The entire hunting process is illustrated on the walls of the Lascaux Caves. The story of the hunt starts from the left and ends on the right with the capture of the prey. Exactly how images are pieced together in a comic strip!

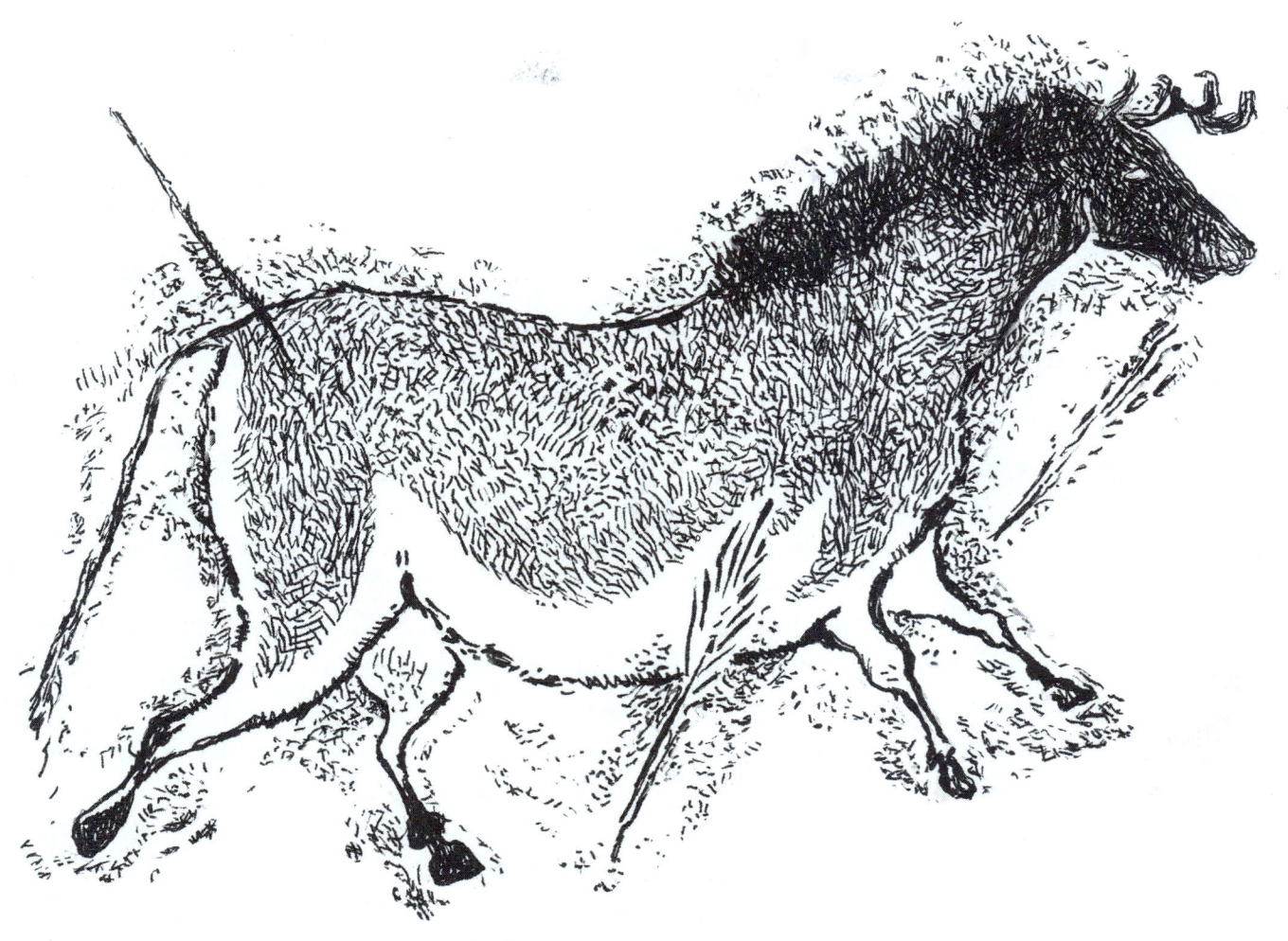

Cave painting of a dun (brownish) horse, mid-hunt, at Lascaux

realized that some plants, rocks and minerals left dyed stains when rubbed on to something. If you visit any such cave and observe carefully, you'll see that the colour palette—or the range of colours that these artists chose—mostly consisted of earthy tones, like yellows, ochres, reds, whites and greens. And, believe it or not, these early artists also *made* colours. It's true! They ground the minerals in a mortar made from a hollowed stone with a pestle made of animal bone. The pigment obtained was then mixed with animal fat, egg yolk, water and even blood (ew!) to make the paste with which they painted. Then they applied the paint on the walls in a variety of ways—using brushes made of twigs, animal hair or fibrous plants, or just their fingers, with which they smeared or dabbed the colours.

Prehistoric Art Galleries in India

India has about 5000 prehistoric cave art sites that take us back in time and into the world of our ancestors. Edakkal in Kerala, Piklihal and Tekkalkota in Karnataka, Bhimbetka and Jogimara in Madhya Pradesh, Kupgallu in Telangana and Lakhudiyar in Uttarakhand are some of these art galleries of the ancient world, where you can witness the splendour of prehistoric art.

It is believed that the oldest of Indian cave paintings are in Bhimbetka, which were done around 30,000 years ago. Just like Lascaux, the Bhimbetka Caves too were found by accident. In 1957, an archaeologist named Dr Vishnu Wakankar was on a train from Bhopal to Itarsi in Madhya Pradesh. He was gazing out of the window at the passing scenery when a series of low hills caught his eye. His instincts told him that these hills were very old and needed to be explored. Following his archaeological hunch, Dr Wakankar got off the train at the next station and went back to examine the hills. As he wandered through the densely forested terrain, he found himself amid caves decorated with paintings in a style that appeared pretty ancient. A few days later, Dr Wakankar returned to the site with his team and discovered about 700 caves, out of which 400 housed prehistoric paintings!

If you have read the Mahabharata, you can probably guess where the name 'Bhimbetka' comes from. Bhimbetka owes its name to the second Pandava brother, Bheem, who appears in the epic about warring cousins—the Pandavas and the Kauravas—who fought a great and terrible war in Kurukshetra many, many years ago. It is believed that when the five Pandava brothers were banished from their kingdom by the Kauravas, Bheem came to live in these caves. Hence, the caves are named after him.

Surrounded by evergreen forests and hillocks, these caves, or rather rock shelters, became the perfect studios for prehistoric artists. (In case you're wondering, rock shelters are different from caves since they are smaller openings at the base of a rock or an overhanging cliff face.) Animals and birds, such as bison, tigers, rhinos, elephants, boars, monkeys and peacocks, are the chief subjects of these paintings, though there are also depictions of men hunting and some religious ceremonies too. The Bhimbetka Caves also provide the earliest evidence of music and dance in prehistoric times, since many paintings in these rock shelters depict human figures dancing! Done in reds and greens and whites of all hues and varieties, the humans in these paintings are drawn as stick figures, but the animals are shown more realistically—powerful and full-bodied.

But perhaps the most fascinating aspect of these paintings is that not only did the cavemen in Bhimbetka draw what they saw but also what they imagined. There is a drawing of a cow in one of the rock shelters, for example, which shows two baby calves inside it! Then there's a rock shelter, popularly called the Zoo Rock, which shows many different animals grouped together, such as the elephant, the bison and the sambar deer. Imagine an entire zoo illustrated on one rock!

What's more, it seems that people from various eras used the Bhimbetka Caves as their canvas, and hence there are many layers of paintings on their surfaces, one on top of the other. Each layer allows a peek into the everyday life of the people of a particular period. The later paintings, for example, show somewhat different themes than what we see in the earlier paintings. Instead of the powerful animals, skilful hunters and pretty dancers of an older time, these depict armoured men, royal processions and horse-drawn chariots. From this we can assume that the later paintings—dated about 10,000 years from today—were drawn much after the Stone Age had ended and a more settled way of life had begun.

A Recap: Our Arty Ancestors

The paintings on the ancient natural canvasses were spontaneous and untrained, yet extremely dynamic and powerful. Cave paintings are among the greatest gifts left behind for us by our ancestors. The study of these primitive paintings by the very first artists of the world gives us a rare glimpse into the lives of the early humans; it tells us the stories of our evolution. These oldest signs of human creativity, in simple forms and graceful lines, amaze and inspire even today.

Catch the Real Thing!

Bhimbetka Caves
A UNESCO World Heritage Site

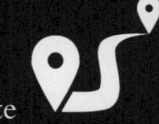

Where: Madhya Pradesh (46 km south of Bhopal)

Entry: Rs 10 for Indian nationals; Rs 100 for foreign nationals

What to see: Don't worry, these caves are not the deep, dark, bat-infested chambers you're imagining them to be! Look for Zoo Rock (Shelter 4) as well as Auditorium Rock (Shelter 3). The latter has cup-shaped depressions on its surface, called cupules. Archaeologists believe that the rock surface was scooped out for ritualistic purposes. You should also visit Shelter 15, which features a splendid red bison.

Remember: There are no refreshment facilities here, so do carry water.

Know more at: www.mptourism.com

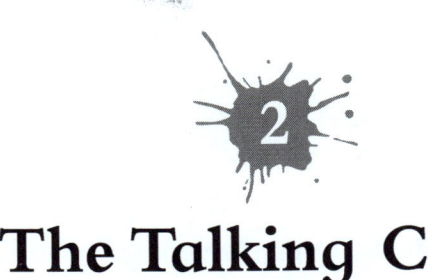

The Talking Caves

Ajanta and Ellora

Let's Walk through Ajanta

The Lucky Tiger

On a bright summer morning of 1819, a British hunting group led by Captain John Smith—a young officer from the Madras Presidency—set out on an expedition in the thick jungles of the Sahyadri Hills near Aurangabad in Maharashtra. The men walked gingerly through the majestic wilderness that was shrouded in mystery while keeping their eyes peeled for game. And then it happened—the savage growl of a tiger pierced the quiet of the jungle!

Captain Smith quickly ordered all his men to follow him through the rocky bed of River Waghora and walked towards the cliff from where the sound seemed to have come. The hunting party was hopping from one rock to the other, when the captain suddenly stopped in his tracks. The paw prints of the tiger led straight to a cave before them. But this was no ordinary cave; it didn't seem like a natural cave created by a river. There was something different about this one. And then realization dawned upon Captain Smith: he was standing in front of a cave that was created by humans, carved perfectly out of huge rocks.

Captain Smith fashioned a torch out of some dried grass and lit it as he entered the yawning cave, which was enveloped in tangled creepers and thick undergrowth. He saw a long hall with pillars on either side, which led to a Buddhist stupa, a dome-shaped shrine. When he held aloft his make-do torch, he saw the most elaborate paintings on the walls of the cave. He had chanced upon art that had been lying hidden in the jungle, far from the human eye, for who knows how long! As the stunned captain advanced towards the far end of the hall, he brought out a hunting knife from his pocket and carved his name on the wall. (Something one should NEVER EVER do in a historical site!)

Captain John Smith had unearthed the most beautiful cave paintings of Asia. He had discovered the Ajanta Caves. And well, a tiger was saved too!

The Secrets of Ajanta

A discovery such as this cannot remain a secret for very long. Soon word spread and many archaeologists and historians thronged the caves, and together they found some thirty caves in Ajanta. The one that Captain Smith had discovered is now called Cave 10 and stands in the centre of the face of the cliff.

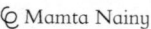

But what's so special about a bunch of old caves, you ask? Well, if you've read the previous chapter, everything! For starters, the Ajanta Caves are not natural but *man-made* caves. The world over, they are considered the most magnificent surviving art galleries from the ancient world. Even today, many of the paintings in these caves enchant viewers with their original colours: lampblack, vivid red, indigo blue, chalk white and more. The Ajanta Caves, illustrated with marvellous artworks that are composed in masterful strokes, are one of the finest examples of Indian art and architecture. The caves are rich with striking depictions of lifelike figures bearing tranquil facial features. It can be said that there was nothing as refined or sophisticated before the Ajanta paintings were created, and they've influenced the artistic traditions of not just India but other South Asian countries as well.

The caves are home to engravings too. The oldest of the caves in Ajanta have inscriptions dating back to the second century BCE! If you were wondering, inscriptions are writings or symbols carved indelibly on monuments. This was how messages were spread long before emails, SMSs and Facebook . . . Talk about hard work!

The history of the marvellous Ajanta Caves has been traced back to the great Indian emperor Asoka. It is said that during the third century BCE, the Buddhist emperor of the Mauryan dynasty wanted to bring to his people the teachings of Gautama Buddha and appeal to them to practise tolerance and non-violence. And so he sent his monks far and wide with this message— all the way to Maharashtra from his kingdom of Magadha in southern Bihar. The monks began to explore and excavate the Sahyadri Hills—the mountainside above River Waghora—to erect monasteries (viharas) and prayer halls (*chaityas*). It is believed that the monks didn't travel in the monsoons, and during their stay in the caves, they put their time and creativity to good use by following artistic pursuits.

A 400-Year-Long Break

One of the most intriguing facts about the Ajanta Caves is that, in 100 BCE, this unique art project was paused for a period of some 400 years!

Studies show that the excavations of the horseshoe-shaped valley of River Waghora were undertaken in two phases by the monks: the first was around the second century BCE and the second, between the fourth and sixth centuries CE. So for around 100 years, the monks continued working on the Ajanta Caves, but the project was suddenly abandoned, marking the end of phase one. Centuries later, another set of monks came back to finish the project.

Now the million-dollar question: why such a long break? Did the monks think they needed to gain more knowledge about the Buddha? After all, they had to get their facts right if they were depicting his life and teachings in these caves. Or could it be that they stalled their work to travel abroad—as far as Egypt and Greece—to learn new artistic techniques from the natives? Or was there a political reason because of which they were summoned back to Magadha? Well, whatever the reasons, when the work was resumed, it continued for another 500 years. Can you imagine the scale

HOW TO PAINT ROCKS WITH ROCKS

Have you ever painted rocks with rocks? No? Well, lucky for you, it's a piece of rock . . . er, cake! Here are the easy steps:

1. On your next vacation, comb any hillside for red, yellow and brown ochre mineral rocks. If you are in northern India, you can even get hold of lapis lazuli (a deep-blue semi-precious stone) for its vibrant colour.

2. Crush the different-coloured mineral rocks and the lapis lazuli separately.

3. Mix each bit of powder with something gluey, like gum or even animal or vegetable fat.

4. There! You're now ready to paint your rock with rocks!

Oh, and don't forget to catch hold of a squirrel's tail for your brush! Nah, just kidding!

of this massive project that it took so long to complete and, in the end, gave us one of the greatest works of art that history has ever seen?

Symbol Speak

Did you know that the caves of Ajanta are numbered serially, and not according to the date of their excavation? What's even more interesting is that the early creations, both paintings and sculptures, do not show the figure of the Buddha. This is because the early Buddhists believed that the Buddha didn't want his image to be worshipped. He wanted people to only follow his teachings. And so, in the paintings of the early period, instead of the figure of the Buddha, symbols related to the life of the Buddha and Buddhist philosophy were used, like the lotus, the elephant, the wheel, etc.

However, in the later works, the Buddha is represented in human form. These paintings also mostly comprise flora and fauna; gods and mythical beings, such as the celestial maidens called apsaras; and pot-bellied *yakshas*, or the caretakers of hidden treasures in the natural

Symbols and Signs

In Buddhism, this is what the following symbols mean:

- **White elephant:** It's believed that the Buddha's mother, Queen Maya, saw a white elephant entering her womb in a dream the night before she conceived the great one. Therefore, a white elephant is regarded as the symbol of good luck and nobility in Buddhism.
- **Lotus:** The white elephant that the Buddha's mother saw in her dream was holding a white lotus in its trunk— a symbol of purity and wisdom.
- **Wheel:** Now, before you think that the white elephant was standing on a wheel, know that's *not* the case. (That would be stretching it a little too far!) The wheel is the symbol of dharma, or the right conduct.

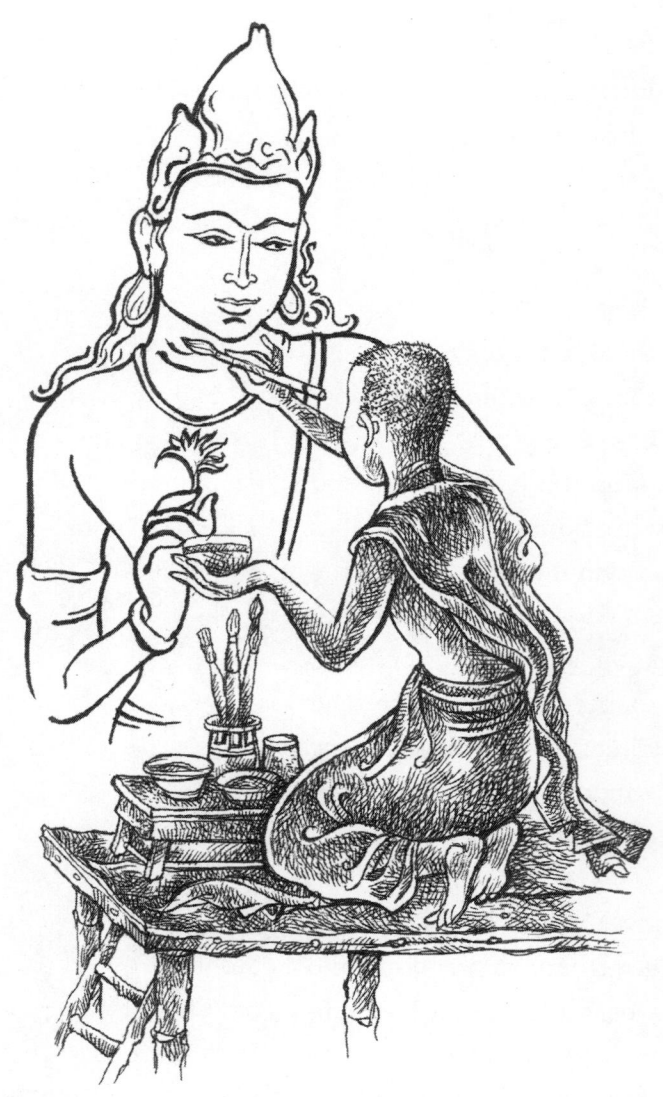

A monk putting the finishing touches to the bodhisattva Padmapani at Ajanta

world. (The last group was perhaps included to provide some comic relief.) Many of the caves here also depict scenes from the Jataka tales—ancient stories of the Buddha's previous lives, brought to life with the help of various talking animals. These paintings also depict the bodhisattvas, who are basically divine beings in Buddhism that help humans by leading them to the path of kindness and compassion.

On one of the walls of Cave 17, for example, the episode 'Mahakapi Jataka' is depicted in pictorial form. In this story, the Buddha appears as a bodhisattva monkey, who saves the life of a hunter by rescuing him from a deep pit. But when the hunter is hungry, he tries to kill the same monkey for food. The bodhisattva monkey then makes the hunter realize how selfish he's been in wanting to kill the creature that saved his life.

There's another very powerful painting in Cave 10. Here, a depiction of 'Shyama Jataka' shows the Buddha in one of his previous births as a forest dweller named Shyama, who tirelessly takes care of his blind parents. One day, when Shyama goes to fetch some water for his parents, the king of Kashi, who was on a hunting expedition, mistakes him for a boar and shoots him with a poisoned arrow. Later, the king is shocked to discover that he's injured a man by mistake. Deeply sorry, he goes to Shyama's parents to seek their forgiveness and leads them to where their son lies dying. Shyama's parents wail uncontrollably at the agony of their wounded son. Then, out of compassion, the god Indra pours the elixir of life in Shyama's mouth, which revives him. Not only does the god save Shyama's life, he also restores the eyesight of the blind parents! A few scenes of this tale are depicted in Cave 17 as well.

The drawings of these stories follow a sort of pattern: Sometimes they flow from top to bottom and at others, from bottom to top. Some even flow from left to right—just like a comic strip!—and also from right to left. So as you walk around the caves and follow the actions and expressions of the people portrayed in the paintings, you can actually see the stories come alive.

Crack the Ajanta Technique

The colours used in the paintings at Ajanta were obtained from the rocks available in the surrounding hills. For the yellows, reds and ochres, a type of natural clay was used; for the black, lampblack; and for the whites, lime. Interestingly, the monks devised an ingenious new technique to apply these dyes: First, a rough mud plaster, containing mud, cow dung, grit and animal hair, was pressed on to the walls of the caves. Then the surface was coated with a layer of fine lime wash, after which the colours were finally applied. This age-old method is now called tempera.

There's a three-dimensional quality to the paintings at Ajanta. Not only are the human, animal and bird figures drawn masterfully with the perfect use of lines and strokes, but human emotions in the facial features, like love, greed and compassion, have also been expertly captured by the artists. The costumes, jewellery and hairstyles are also drawn with immense care and recreate the time in which the subjects of these paintings lived.

The Curious Case of the Curse of the Caves

Well, this little story may be of interest to many: it is widely believed that there's a charm around the Ajanta Caves! So the tale goes that anyone who tries to deface the paintings in any way or reproduce them is struck by bad luck. Mysteriously, many attempts to make copies of these paintings and then exhibit them in museums have been highly unsuccessful. In most of these cases, either the museums at which they were to be exhibited caught fire and the canvasses were destroyed, or the curator (the one who is in charge of the works of art in a museum) went insane! Unbelievable, right?

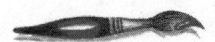

Time to Explore Ellora

A Blending of Faiths

Just about 100 kilometres from the Ajanta Caves is another cluster of man-made caves. Created almost 1000 years after Ajanta, these are the Ellora Caves. However, unlike Ajanta, these were never 'lost' and later 'found' given their close proximity to Dakshinapatha—an ancient trade route in the Indian subcontinent, linking the western seaports to the great southern states. So traders, merchants, monks, rulers and foreign travellers constantly visited and wrote about these caves well into the nineteenth century.

Extending over two kilometres, the thirty-four caves of Ellora were built during the sixth and ninth centuries CE under the rule of the Kalachuri, Chalukya and Rashtrakuta dynasties. Curiously, these caves house temples as well as monasteries. There are twelve Buddhist, seventeen Hindu and five Jain caves at Ellora, which shows the religious harmony of the time. The caves are numbered chronologically, starting with the Buddhist caves at the south, proceeding to the Hindu caves at the centre and ending at the Jain caves towards the north. Across all the caves, you can find depictions of mythical scenes as well as Buddhist, Jain and Hindu gods.

The Hindu caves are the most elaborate in design, with several unique artworks as well as intricate panels and carvings displaying scenes from the Hindu epics and the Puranas. Characterized by dynamism and drama, these caves are grand in their size, design and the variety of subjects depicted in them. The Buddhist caves are mostly composed of viharas, which were created primarily as secluded spaces for study and worship. These caves have images of Gautama Buddha and bodhisattvas in simple forms, and also include cooking and living spaces as well as sleeping cells (something like sleeping bunkers) for travelling monks. The Jain caves are not very large but contain detailed carvings and paintings that depict the Jain chronicles. These caves have images of Jain *tirthankara*s (the great teachers), like Gomateshvara, Parasnath and Mahavira, surrounded by lush flora and fauna.

The Elaborate Shrine of Ellora

The most famous temple in Ellora is the Kailash Temple (Cave 16), dedicated to the Hindu god Shiva. In the eighth century CE, the Rashtrakuta king Krishna I, who was a great devotee of Lord Shiva, commanded his architects to recreate the Himalayan abode of Lord Shiva—Mount Kailash. And so, over a period of 150 years, 7000 labourers carved out a thirty-metre-tall, multi-storey temple complex from a single rock! Considered to be the largest and most significant rock-cut temple in India, it is said that the highly skilled sculptors appointed by the king scooped out 4,00,000 tons of rock to create the temple, and that they did it only with chisels, hammers and their bare hands!

The temple complex has four main parts: a double-storey entryway; the shrine of Lord Shiva's divine mount, Nandi; the main temple;

Rock-Cut Treasures across India

A combination of architecture and sculpture, the tradition of rock-cut temples in India goes back a long time. Some of these cave-temples include the Elephanta, Bhaja, Kanheri and Karla Caves in Maharashtra; the Udayagiri and Khandagiri Caves in Odisha; the Badami Caves in Karnataka; the Barabar Caves in Bihar; and the Bagh Caves in Madhya Pradesh.

and five minor shrines around a large courtyard. The base of the main temple shows a carved row of graceful elephants that makes it look like the majestic creatures are holding the whole temple aloft.

The courtyard of the complex has huge pillared arcades that house enormous sculptures of various gods and goddesses. Lord Shiva himself is depicted in sixty-four different poses in the sculptures! The most remarkable of these is the grand sculpture of the demon king Ravana trying to shake Mount Kailash with all his might as Lord Shiva pins him down with his big toe.

What else, you ask? The temple also has bridges connecting one part to another, underground passages, balconies and stairways, and even sophisticated rainwater harvesting systems!

The scale of the structures in the Kailash Temple, with its larger-than-life deities, is so immense that one feels *tiny* standing in front of them. An inscription on one of the temple walls says that when it was being built, even the celestial beings in the skies were struck by its enormity, and that even the artists and architects of the temple couldn't believe that it was them who'd created it! Fascinating, isn't it? Has this ever happened to you—that you created something and couldn't believe it was *you* who'd made such an amazing thing?

A Recap: The 'A' of Indian Art

The Ajanta and Ellora Caves are colossal works of art, each of which attracts more than 5000 visitors every day. And that's because the artists of these magnificent caves not only had an evolved artistic sense and supreme skill, but also a great vision that leaves us spellbound even today. These artists didn't seek any credit for the majestic art they created; there are no names inscribed on the paintings or on the sculptures. For them, the message they wanted to convey was the most important: the message of kindness and humanity, of tolerance and non-violence, depicted through the many stories they immortalized on the rocks of Ajanta and Ellora. Isn't that a pretty cool reason to create art?

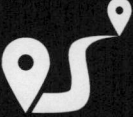

Catch the Real Thing!

Ajanta and Ellora Caves
UNESCO World Heritage Sites

Where: Near Aurangabad, Maharashtra
- **Ajanta:** 107 km from Aurangabad
- **Ellora:** 30 km from Aurangabad

Entry: Rs 30 for Indian nationals; Rs 500 for foreign nationals; free admission for children below fifteen years of age

What to see:
- **Ajanta:** Caves 1, 2, 16 and 17 are must-sees and the best preserved of all.
- **Ellora:** The star attraction is the Kailash Temple (Cave 16). You can also stop at Daulatabad Fort on your way to Ellora!

Remember:
- Don't use the flash of your camera when inside the caves as the light can harm the paintings.
- A long neck is a must to admire these massive works of art!

Know more at:
www.maharashtratourism.gov.in

Small Wonders, Big Wow

Mughal Miniatures

The Emperor and the Arts

Babur Says, 'Hello, Delhi!'

It was the India of 1526. The sound of hoofs ushered in a new dynasty to rule the land. Waves upon waves of men on horseback, led by a fierce-looking leader riding a grandly decorated dark stallion, entered Delhi as a huge line-up of sentries bowed low with their hands on their chests—so low that their noses almost touched the ground—to welcome the new emperor of India.

Zahir-ud-din Muhammad Babur—ruler of Fergana (in present-day Uzbekistan) and descendant of the formidable houses of Timur and Genghis Khan—had entered Delhi. Having fought a fierce battle with the last sultan of Delhi, Ibrahim Lodi, in Panipat, Babur was here to set up his mighty kingdom in India—the Mughal Empire. Babur was a ferocious commander, who was true to his name (you see, *babur* means 'tiger' in Persian) and his reign in India was full of conquests. His empire soon straddled a huge expanse of the Indian subcontinent, and the Mughals ended up ruling it for over three centuries.

But Babur's reign wasn't all war and violence. He was a great patron, or sponsor, of architecture, and was himself a poet and a scholar. During his time, many mosques and monuments were built in India. The Mughal emperor wasn't much impressed with the structures built by the Lodi kings before him; he felt they were not very symmetrical in design. And so, he brought over artisans from Central Asia, who worked with Indian craftsmen to lend uniformity to the buildings Babur wanted erected. Hence, it could be said that the Mughal style of art and architecture that you see in India even today was first introduced by Babur.

A great admirer of proportion and symmetry, Babur commissioned enduring monuments, most of which show a structured, geometric design, with a central dome, slim minarets and large doorways. The three famous mosques built during this time include the Kabuli Bagh Mosque in Panipat, Haryana, which was constructed to mark Babur's victory in the First Battle of Panipat; the Babri Masjid in Ayodhya, Uttar Pradesh; and the Jama Masjid in Sambhal, also in Uttar Pradesh. Babur also wanted to recreate the lush gardens of Fergana in India. So he laid out plans for some exquisite grounds, some of them adorned with pools, reservoirs, fountains and canals. To mark his first major victory after establishing Mughal rule in India—against Rana Sanga of Mewar—Babur laid out the Garden of Victory and a palace called Jal-Mahal (Water Palace) at the edge of Lake Sikri in Fatehpur Sikri. He also built Aram Bagh (Garden of Leisure) by the banks of River Yamuna in Agra, which is said to be the oldest Mughal garden in India.

However, Babur couldn't contribute much to the sphere of art and architecture in India as he fell seriously ill just after four years of his rule here, and died at the age of forty-seven, leaving his large empire to his son. However, by this time the seeds of the Mughal style of art and architecture had been successfully sown in India.

A lot of what we know about Babur today comes from his autobiography, *Baburnama*. Almost everything about his life since his rule over Fergana has been recorded in this book. Babur wrote about a range of things in his book: his battles and conquests, the snow-capped mountains and tall trees of Fergana, his many travels, the lavish parties he threw, the juicy fruits he ate, the exotic birds and animals he saw, his views on what it means to be a good king and about his time in India. And the most wonderful thing about India, Babur says in his book, is that it's a huge country with lots and lots of gold and money! This fascinating memoir, which was originally written in the now extinct Chagatai language, was later translated into Persian on orders of Babur's grandson Akbar, who even had this book illustrated with intricate drawings to accompany the text. It is said that many artists worked on the 141 complex paintings that are in this book, which show battle scenes, grand feasts and natural wonders, among other things.

Humayun, the (Un)Fortunate One

'The fortunate one'—that's what the name of Babur's son Nasir-ud-din Muhammad Humayun means. But in reality, he was far from fortunate! From the time he ascended the throne, after his father's death, Humayun was plagued by problems. Not ambitious like his father, he disliked war and bloodshed. After ruling the empire in India for about a decade, he was defeated in a battle against the Afghan chieftain Sher Shah Suri. Humayun fled to Persia (present-day Iran) and took shelter at his cousin Shah Tahmasp's court. But he returned to India after fifteen long years . . . Guess what he brought back with himself? No, not an exotic Persian carpet. Take another guess.

Nope, not even the super aromatic Persian saffron. Here it is: Humayun brought with him two master painters from his cousin's royal studio in Persia—Mir Sayyid Ali and Abdus Samad. Who can tell if Humayun knew then that by doing so he was laying down the foundation of Mughal art in India!

Humayun was very encouraging of Mir Sayyid Ali and Abdus Samad, and it was from these two artists that he and his son Akbar took lessons in drawing. Talk about learning from the best! These Persian artists collaborated with the native Indian painters who were serving at the royal court at that time, blending the features of Persian art, like fine calligraphy (stylized writing), decorative margins and painted binding, with the emotional appeal and naturalism of Indian artistic traditions. During Humayun's reign, a book of poetry called *Khamsa* (Five Poems), penned by the famous Persian poet Nizami Ganjavi, was illustrated with thirty-four small paintings.

However, in spite of his best efforts and keen interest in art, Humayun could not commission many fine paintings in India during his time. Why, you ask? Well, because, uncannily enough, Humayun too died young—just like his father.

His resting place, Humayun's Tomb—which was commissioned by his wife Bega Begum and built during his son Akbar's reign—still stands tall as a fine example of Mughal architecture in Delhi. This one-of-a-kind memorial was designed by a

Buried in Books

There's quite a story behind Humayun's untimely death. He was very fond of reading and would spend a large part of his day stationed in his huge library. One day, only a few months after he'd regained the throne in India, Humayun was reading his favourite book in his library. He was so engrossed in the text that he completely forgot about his evening prayers. Suddenly, upon hearing the azan (the call for prayer), he rushed down a flight of stairs and tumbled to his death!

Persian architect in such a way that it appears as if it's floating on the well-manicured gardens! Humayun's Tomb was the first Mughal monument in India to feature the distinct Mughal style of the Persian double-dome design, a white marble exterior and Rajasthani decorative elements like *chattri*s (small canopies) and jali (latticework).

Akbar's Mighty Miniatures

Jalal-ud-din Muhammad Akbar, Humayun's son, claimed the throne after defeating a general named Hemu, who'd crowned himself king after Humayun's death. Akbar was only thirteen at that time. Gradually he began strengthening his political control and built his capital at Fatehpur Sikri near Agra in Uttar Pradesh. Since he had to take over the reins of power quite early on, Akbar didn't even get the time to learn how to read and write. But he didn't let this stop him from being keenly interested in and learning about various art forms. In fact, he was known as a great patron of the arts, and so during his reign, hundreds of artists thronged Akbar's royal studios—papermakers, calligraphers, painters, bookbinders—all producing an assortment of works for the royalty.

From the fusion of the Indian and Persian styles of fine art, thanks to the two Persian teachers brought by Humayun as well as the Mughal throne's Timurid legacy, developed a unique Mughal style called miniature paintings during Akbar's reign. These were small-sized or mini paintings—about half the size of a page of this book! Talk about an eye for detail! Have you ever tried painting a detailed landscape complete with an ornate border on a *very* small piece of paper? Try it . . . it's quite a task!

While the original Persian style of miniatures was not very realistic and used fixed settings—similar to posing in an indoor studio—Akbar encouraged the artists in his royal studio to experiment and apply naturalism in their work. He was a great fan of the outdoors and wanted his painters to create paintings that looked 'real' and recreated detailed observations of the natural world around them. And so all the painters in Akbar's court worked together industriously on these miniatures, making sure that the numerous manuscripts were exquisitely illustrated with this natural style of art. The miniature painters created these paintings either in the form of illustrations in books or as leaves in imperial albums that carried portraits of the emperor, courtiers and holy men. They were hardly ever framed and hung on walls. Perhaps the most important miniatures done during Akbar's time were for *Hamzanama*—a collection of stories about Prophet Muhammad's uncle Amir Hamza—which had about 1400 illustrations! The natural surroundings—birds, trees, flowers and mountains—done in vivid, flat colours, like red, yellow, green, orange and blue, look very real in these artworks. Perhaps Akbar perfected his favourite style of 'real' paintings after all!

Faces, Faces Everywhere

Mughal miniature paintings were developed under the patronage or sponsorship of Mughal emperors and, therefore, a large number of these paintings are portraits of Mughal royalty.

The miniature artists mostly created the portraits in side profile (the face as seen from the side), but these were not side profiles in the strictest sense as they showed three-fourths of the face, which is between the front and side views.

These finely detailed drawings, done in bright colours, along with the accompanying calligraphic text, give us the rare opportunity to see and imagine the true likeness of the Mughal emperors who lived centuries ago!

Akbar's love for miniature paintings can also be seen in the beautiful books he commissioned or undertook to be painted during his reign: *Akbarnama*, the official diary of Akbar written by his close friend and adviser Abul Fazl; *Razam Nama,* the Persian translation of the Mahabharata; *Anwar-i-Suhaili,* a book of fables; and *Baburnama,* the chronicles of Akbar's grandfather, Babur. These were all illustrated with miniature paintings under his patronage. These miniatures were so painstakingly intricate and included so many minute details that the painting brushes were made using only a couple of hairs of a squirrel's tail! Can you imagine painting with a brush that has only *two* bristles?

As for the artistic process, the painters first carefully polished the paper with stone or seashell for shine and only then did they start drawing on it. The paper was then coated with a white pigment on which they painted using natural colours. And finally, real gold (yes, you read that right!) was used in the paintings wherever necessary. Offering a dazzling glimpse into the splendour and the riches of the royal courts, these paintings depict the lives of the Mughal kings and queens—their fancy costumes and impressive jewellery; their gruesome wars and victories; the elaborate court scenes and colourful celebrations; and the varied wildlife around them.

Many miniatures done in these years have gained popularity over time. The most famous include *The Defeat of Hemu,* which features in *Akbarnama* and illustrates the Second Battle of Panipat, fought between Akbar and Hemu. Doubling as one of the best bird studies done during Akbar's time is *Bird Catching at Baran* from *Baburnama,* which shows a bird-trapper in Baran, Afghanistan, hiding behind a tree after having spread his net near a lotus pond, where hoopoes, snipes, sarus cranes and other waterbirds have gathered to drink water. Another well-known painting in the style shows Abul Fazl presenting the first copy of *Akbarnama* to Emperor Akbar in court amid great pomp and splendour. This painting is somewhat like a photograph in that it captures a memorable moment.

Under Akbar's patronage, the imperial studios grew in number and many artists entered the court to study the Mughal style of painting. However, it was only under the direction of Jahangir, Akbar's son, that Mughal miniature painting reached its peak. How? Let's find out!

The Art and Animal-Lover Called Jahangir

The fourth Mughal emperor of India, Nur-ud-din Beig Mohammad Khan Salim, aka Jahangir, also took great interest in art. He loved painting and was fascinated by the beauty of nature. During his time, court scenes, royal receptions, hunting scenes and wildlife became the major themes of the Mughal paintings. The artists during this time became specialists, such that some painted only animals, some only did portraits, while some others were experts at painting court scenes. Interestingly, the miniature paintings of this period were bound together in big albums called *muraqqa*s. Can you imagine such a sketchbook, filled with beautifully intricate mini paintings? Another feature of

The Curious King

After dinner every night, Jahangir used to drink a full glass of camel milk. Once it so happened that he liked the milk of one particular camel so much that the next day, he asked his minister to find out what food this camel ate. Jahangir was extremely curious about animals, so of course the matter didn't end there—Jahangir had the same food prepared and given to his entire herd of camels!

Jahangir's reign was that portraiture, or portrait painting, occupied much of the artists' time in the royal studios and thus very few books were illustrated. The Mughal emperor also preferred that a single painter worked on one painting rather than a group, as was the practice during his father's time.

Among the finest artworks of Jahangir's time are elaborate court scenes that show him surrounded by scores of courtiers—and each and every figure in the painting is drawn realistically! Jahangir's ascent to the throne, his durbar or court and his meetings with the royal visitors have all been documented in these paintings. Abul Hasan, Ustad Mansur, Bishandas and Daulat were some of the most well-known painters in Jahangir's royal court.

The Mughal emperor really adored animals, especially rare species, so much so that he had his very own personal zoo! It may sound odd, but it was quite ordinary for kings to have personal zoos in those days. A story goes that one day, a new exotic animal—a zebra—was presented to Jahangir by the Turks as special gift from Abyssinia. The emperor could not believe his eyes as he observed this unusual creature. He thought that the stripes had been *painted* on the zebra . . . imagine! (You see, we were still quite a few centuries away from Animal Planet or the Discovery Channel.) Sceptical, he asked his men to find out whether the stripes were real or not and, after much investigation, he was finally convinced that the zebra's stripes had been created by none other than God Himself! Jahangir then asked his royal artist Ustad Mansur to replicate the animal realistically on paper. He was so taken by the zebra that he even mentioned it in his memoir, *Jahangirnama*.

Sometime during his reign, Jahangir came in contact with British royalty and received some oil paintings from England as gifts. The European style of painting greatly influenced him and he encouraged the painters in his royal studios to emulate the Western artists. Therefore, if you observe the paintings from this time, you will notice that the brushwork became finer and the palette, lighter. A very interesting example of this is a portrait of Jahangir done by one of the most renowned

Animals Galore

Many animals and birds became the subjects of miniatures done during Jahangir's time. Ustad Mansur, Jahangir's favourite wildlife painter, drew many realistic paintings of animals and birds, such as the dodo, the chameleon, the turkey cock, the barbet and the pheasant.

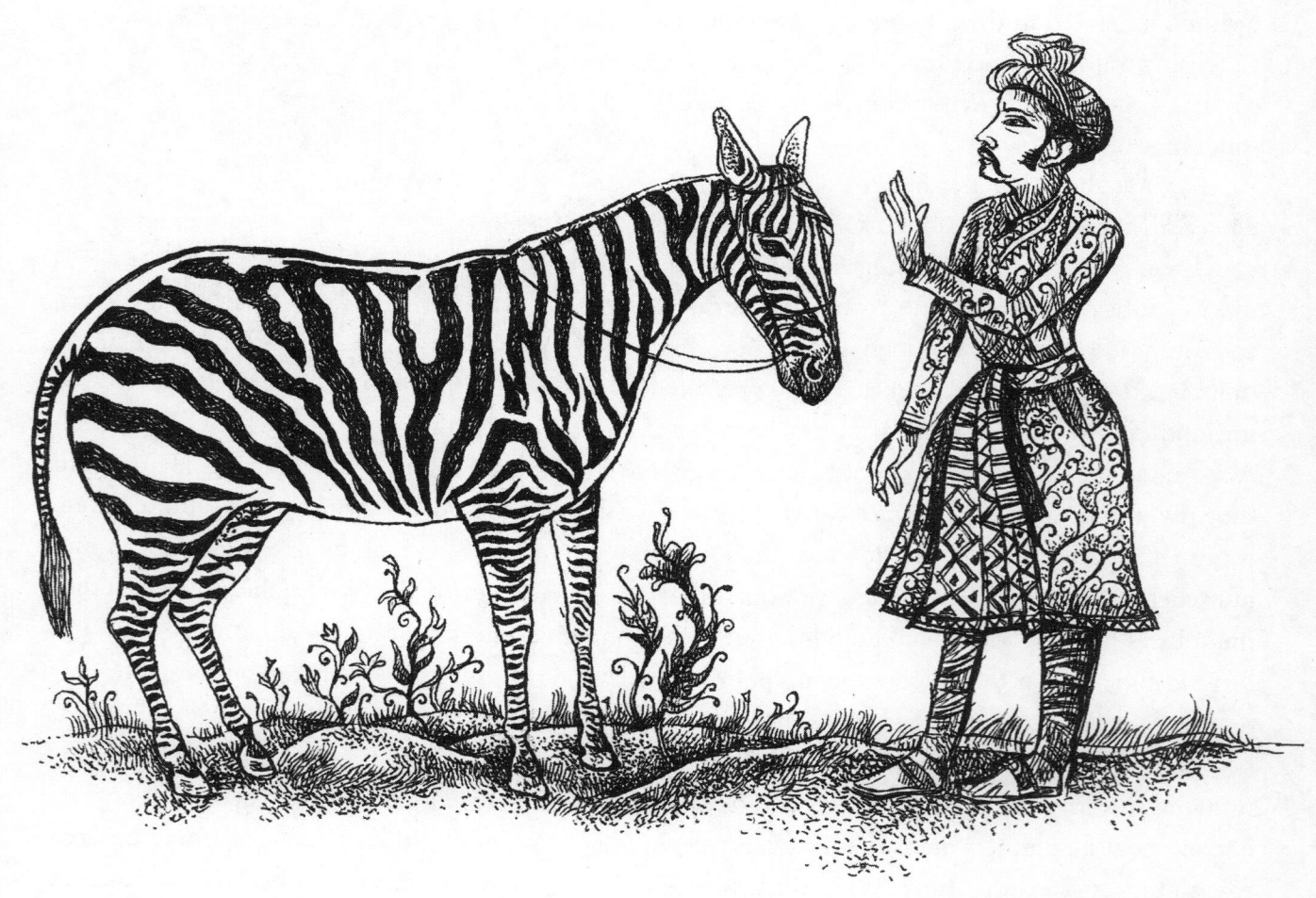

Jahangir just can't wrap his head around the stripes of the enigmatic zebra

portrait artists of Jahangir's court—Abul Hasan. In this unusual painting, the Mughal emperor is shown holding a picture of the Madonna, or Mary, the mother of Jesus. The portrait, painted in soft colours, is surrounded by calligraphy and decorated borders—a characteristic feature of Mughal miniature paintings.

Did you know that there was *another* great promoter of Mughal art during Jahangir's reign? The Mughal emperor was supported by his eighteenth and last wife, Nur Jahan, in taking Mughal art to greater heights. Herself an artist and poet, Nur Jahan built many monuments and gardens, and even had exquisite coins minted under her name—a first for a woman of her time! She was very encouraging of miniature artists and even created a splendid gallery of miniature paintings in the palace garden. The empress is said to have inspired the architectural style of the legendary Taj Mahal in Agra by building her father's mausoleum, the Tomb of Itmad-ud-Daula, in the same city, which was the first example of intricate marble carvings. After Jahangir's death, Nur Jahan completed a most wonderful marble tomb for her husband, the construction of which had commenced during Jahangir's living years. She also worked towards improving the condition of women in the empire and it was due to her strong influence that portraits of women started appearing in the miniature paintings done during this time.

Wah Taj, Shah Jahan!

Everybody knows about the world-famous marble monument Taj Mahal. After all, it is considered to be one of the greatest monuments of love and one of the best examples of architecture in the world. Did you know that this timeless monument was commissioned by the fifth Mughal emperor, Shahab-ud-din Muhammad Khurram, better known as Shah Jahan, for his beloved wife

Mumtaz Mahal? Shah Jahan was Jahangir's son, who took over the throne when his father's health deteriorated. Considered to be the golden age of the Mughal Empire, Shah Jahan's reign was a prosperous one. Emeralds, sapphires, rubies, diamonds and all sorts of precious stones mined from Indian soil during his time filled up the royal treasury. Just imagine the grandeur!

Shah Jahan is most celebrated today for his architectural developments: Taj Mahal in Agra; Jama Masjid in Delhi; Red Fort in the city of Shahjahanabad (present-day Old Delhi); and a number of palaces and mosques throughout India. With the monuments constructed during his time, Shah Jahan broke away from the rigid, strictly geometric approach to architecture that Babur promoted, and focused more on the beauty and design of the structures. Double domes, a rectangular external gate with an archway inside and lush surroundings with beautiful gardens are typical of the monuments built during Shah Jahan's reign. The designs of these monuments also incorporated the use of delicate details, decorative elements and naturalistic motifs, like the vines and flowers inspired from miniature art. However, Shah Jahan surpassed himself with his most wondrous creation—the Taj Mahal. Its large dome, often called the 'onion dome' because of its colour and shape, the marble walls that were originally studded with precious and semi-precious stones, the detailed calligraphic inscriptions and fantastic floral carvings, the sprawling garden with a reflecting pool, the massive entrance and the exquisite minarets together make it a timeless masterpiece. It's believed that this monument was constructed by 20,000 stone carvers and masons over the course of twenty long years. Did you know it's also rumoured that Shah Jahan chopped off the hands of the workers after they completed the Taj Mahal so that they could not make another such monument? Ouch!

As for fine arts, the Mughal emperor continued encouraging painters and commissioning paintings as before. He also kept alive the miniature painting traditions from Jahangir's time and added several paintings to the magnificent *Emperor's Album* that was passed on to him, also known as *The Shah Jahan Album*. This album was a spectacular collection of detailed paintings, such as nature studies and portraits, created during Jahangir's time. But sadly, Shah Jahan couldn't manage to take his father's tradition forward by much. The portraits done during his time started looking more like statues; they were perfect in technique but quite lifeless in appeal. In fact, during Shah Jahan's time, miniature paintings started weakening.

After years of successful rule, Shah Jahan fell ill, and his four sons started quarrelling over the throne. There were bitter fights, and Shah Jahan's third son, Aurangzeb, eventually seized the throne and declared himself the emperor. He placed his father under house arrest at Agra Fort. Not such a nice thing to do to one's father, right? But such was the time of mighty kings . . . Shah Jahan's only desire was to be given a chamber from where he could see the Taj Mahal every day, and his son obliged. Shah Jahan lived in confinement for nine long years before he breathed his last.

Aurangzeb Abstains from the Arts

Aurangzeb was highly religious and had little interest in fine arts, dance or music. This new emperor was not very encouraging of miniature artists and so only a few portraits were done during his time. He eventually (and sadly) dismissed all the artists from the Mughal court, and even banned music and dance! Under Aurangzeb's rule, the Mughal Empire started losing all its power and glory, and this led to the loss of all its wealth and territory. Soon the mighty Mughal Empire fell, and the once renowned Mughal miniature artists had to move to the northern parts of India to find patronage.

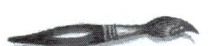

Mini Goes Places

The Rise of the Rajput Miniatures

When the Mughal miniature artists left the Mughal court, the Rajput maharajas of neighbouring regions employed them. This saved the beautiful miniature painting tradition from fading away. Since the painters were now under new kings, a new style began to develop. These paintings came to be known as the Rajput miniatures, with Jaipur, Mewar, Malwa, Jodhpur, Kota, Bundi and Kishangarh in Rajasthan as the main centres of this art form.

Rajput miniatures were done on loose sheets of paper or on the walls of havelis (you know, those massive townhouses or mansions that they show in movies). Bright colours were used during this time, which were handmade and naturally extracted from vegetables, minerals and shells, and even processed from precious stones. The themes

An Indian Mona Lisa

There's one set of paintings that has a special place among the Rajput miniatures—those of the elegant and super graceful Bani Thani!

First created by Nihal Chand, a court painter of Kishangarh, these paintings show an elegant woman in profile, with an exaggerated lengthening of the eyes and nose and a subtle smile on the lips. It's said that the painter was inspired by one of the poems written by Raja Sawant Singh, the king of Kishangarh, which described the beauty of a lady called Bani Thani. So taken was Nihal Chand by this poem that he created a series of paintings based on its subject. The woman's smile in the Bani Thani paintings is often compared to that of Mona Lisa!

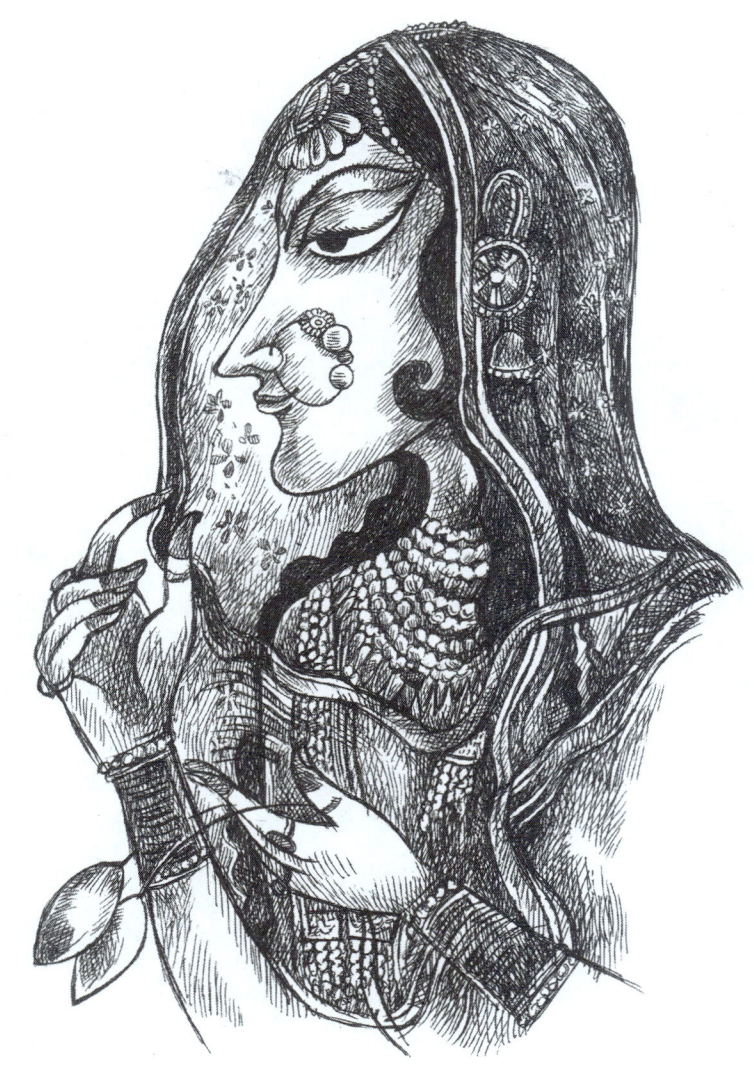

Bani Thani cracks a sweet smile

of these paintings also changed, and the painters started illustrating events from the Mahabharata, the Ramayana, stories from the life of the Hindu god Krishna as well as festivals and processions. The human figures in the Rajput miniatures had sharp features and well-defined facial expressions. The colourful dresses of the figures were usually set against light-coloured buildings or small hillocks to add depth—making it look 3D—and stylized motifs like decorative trees and flowers were also used.

Enter the Pahari School of Art

During the mid-seventeenth century, many artist families moved to the small princely states in the Himalayan foothills, like Jammu, Garhwal, Chamba, Guler, Mandi, Basohli and Kangra, to find new patrons and better living conditions. And this led to the birth of Pahari (*pahar* is Hindi for 'hill') miniature paintings.

The Pahari miniatures are primarily divided into two schools of art: Basohli and Kangra. The Basohli miniatures prospered towards the end of the seventeenth century, and most of these miniatures were exquisite illustrations of Radha–Krishna and other gods and goddesses. This school of art is best known for its bold and brilliant colour schemes, strong lines, sharp profiles with the eyes shaped like lotus petals and an almost three-dimensional depiction of jewellery with raised drops of white.

In the mid-eighteenth century, the popularity of Basohli paintings began to fade and a new style emerged from the hill town of Kangra. These Kangra miniatures were different from the rest as they used delicate lines, freehand movement and calmer colours. While the Basohli artists mostly drew from literary classics like the Ramayana and the Gita Govinda, the main theme of the Kangra miniatures was ancient romantic lore from Hindu mythology, like the stories of Nala–Damayanti and Radha–Krishna.

What's a School of Art?

A school of art refers to a group of like-minded artists who have a similar approach to art. This means they follow the same style, use the same technique and sometimes even have the same teachers. More often than not, a school of art is named after the city or region where these artists live and work.

A Recap: No Mini Feat

The miniatures, though small in size, are beautiful and meticulous paintings. The extravagant Mughal miniature paintings provided inspiration to many future artists and schools, and they continue to inspire even today. We cannot deny credit to the Mughal rulers who encouraged such a fine form of painting and helped it flourish. If it hadn't been for them, such extraordinary art wouldn't have emerged or been developed in India. It seems that the Mughals (well, almost all of them) were as passionate about art and architecture as they were about warfare and expanding their territories!

As you would know by now, each miniature tells a story, be it Mughal or Rajput or Pahari. If you look at these miniatures closely, you can witness the elaborate scenes depicted in the paintings almost coming alive right in front of your eyes—thanks to all the small but fine details. It is as though the artists left behind a stash of photographs for us to find, explore and use to understand the times they lived in!

Catch the Real Thing!

Miniature Paintings

Where: The National Museum, New Delhi

Entry: Rs 20 for Indian nationals; Rs 650 for foreign nationals; free entry for students up to Class 12 with a school identity card

What to see: The National Museum has a collection of over 17,000 miniature paintings! The museum houses various galleries that showcase miniature paintings from different places and times.

Remember: As with your favourite stories or videos, do go back to the paintings you like best again and again. You're sure to find something interesting in the details each time!

Know more at: www.nationalmuseumindia.gov.in

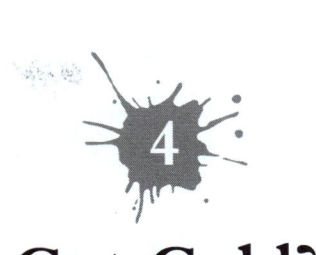

Got Gold?

Tanjore Paintings

Thriving Thanjavur

On the fertile delta of River Kaveri, nestled snugly in the heart of India's southern state of Tamil Nadu, is a fabled city—a city of temples and palaces, a city that served as the capital of the great Chola Empire when it was at the height of its glory, a city that gave birth to the traditional

bobblehead dolls (you know, those roly-poly dolls whose heads wobble with a gentle tap) and other handicrafts. The city of Thanjavur. But there is one more thing that Thanjavur is known for—it is home to one of the most unique and popular painting styles of south India: Tanjore paintings, which are done using gold (yes, you read that right—*real* gold!).

Art Lost and Found

How Tanjore paintings originated makes for one of the most interesting stories in Indian art history. The earliest traces of this painting style can be found on the walls of Thanjavur's Brihadeeshwara Temple, or the Big Temple, dedicated to Lord Shiva, which was built in the eleventh century and is considered the greatest creation of the Chola king Raja Raja I. These paintings, done on the lime-plastered walls of the temple corridors, are among the best works dedicated to Lord Shiva, being unique in their use of lavish gold decorations, especially the crowns and the jewellery of the illustrated gods and goddesses. But, with the fall of the Chola dynasty, the art form was all but forgotten until the fifteenth century.

Interest in this style of art was roused again when Thanjavur became part of the Vijayanagara Empire in the fifteenth century, and, fortunately, the Vijayanagara kings were great patrons of all forms of art. The empire was managed by *nayak*s, or military governors, who too encouraged art, architecture and literature a great deal. During this time, the kings commissioned local artists to decorate the walls and doors of their palaces with depictions of the important events of a king's reign, like his coronation ceremony (the crowning of the heir to the royal throne) or his victories on the battlefield. The kings also ordered the painters to portray some religious themes on the walls and doors of temples, which were mostly inspired from ancient scriptures. There was another specification: these paintings were to be done in the same style as those in the Brihadeeshwara Temple.

And so the artists followed the kings' orders and created ornate paintings in vibrant colours. These paintings also used real gold and were extremely elaborate in their decorative details—their subjects were adorned in clothes with intricate, colourful patterns as well as a variety of ornaments, and they even sported different hairdos, each complete with a fancy beaded accessory! Some of these temple wall paintings can still be seen in Hampi (in present-day Karnataka), which was the capital city of the Vijayanagara Empire, and also in Kanchipuram, Tamil Nadu. As the sixteenth century rolled in, the nayaks, who initially only helped in running the Vijayanagara Empire, became extremely powerful and declared themselves the kings of the empire's territories, including Thanjavur. They continued with the painting traditions of the rulers before them.

But Why Gold?

Painting on the walls of palaces and temples presented a problem—the lighting on these walls was very poor, and so the artwork appeared rather dull (you see, they didn't have spotlights in those days!). To make the breathtakingly beautiful paintings visible to the visitors and devotees, the kings decided that bright colours and glittering gold foil be used. In doing so, the depictions stood out. Another reason behind the use of gold was that, for the artists, the gods reproduced in these paintings were nothing short of the real gods themselves, and so it was important for them to make the paintings similar to the idols in the temples, which housed deities decked out in fine clothing and precious jewellery.

Grander than Grand

The Vijayanagara Empire was said to be greatly abundant in its wealth. It's believed that the Vijayanagara kings weighed themselves against gold and semi-precious stones on special occasions, like solar or lunar eclipses, religious festivals and coronation ceremonies, and donated these items to the temple priests!

Many gold coins were also issued during the Vijayanagara period. An Italian traveller who visited the kingdom commented that the horse belonging to the empire's king was worth more than some Italian cities—simply on account of the ornaments it wore!

The Magic of the Marathas

The temple paintings of the Vijayanagara Empire and Nayak Dynasty gained greatness all right, but it was only with the arrival of the Maratha rulers in the seventeenth and eighteenth centuries—their headquarters being in Thanjavur—that Tanjore paintings attained the glorious form by which we know them today. It all started when the great Maratha warrior king Venkoji, Chhatrapati Shivaji's stepbrother, seized power from the Nayak kings in the late seventeenth century and established Maratha rule in Tamil Nadu. Venkoji was a great lover of art, and he made Thanjavur the cultural epicentre of the South. So it was during his time that Tanjore art really thrived. Then, under the patronage of the second last Maratha king, Serfoji II, Thanjavur's painting traditions prospered even further.

The royal artists during the Maratha rule combined the existing Tanjore style—of amazing details, rich texture and utmost elegance on decorated walls—with elements of the then popular Mughal and Rajput miniature art forms to create an altogether new style in Tanjore art. Apart from painting the walls of palaces and temples, they started making paintings on cloth canvasses pasted on a wooden support. These paintings were then framed and installed in the Maratha palaces and other buildings to enhance their beauty. The subjects of these works were mostly gods and goddesses, and the painters used vibrant colours, like glowing red, deep green, rich blue and shiny white. They highlighted all the details in the paintings—including the clothing, jewellery, thrones, pillars, etc.—with wafer-thin gold foil, raising these designs above the surface and lending the work a carved effect. Almost all the figures in these paintings had round faces and almond-shaped eyes, and the main god or goddess in the centre was shown as being flanked by curtains, arches and ornate borders. As this style of art developed more and more, it became highly lavish. And apart from the gold foil, uncut emeralds, rubies and diamonds too were used in these paintings. Talk about extravagance!

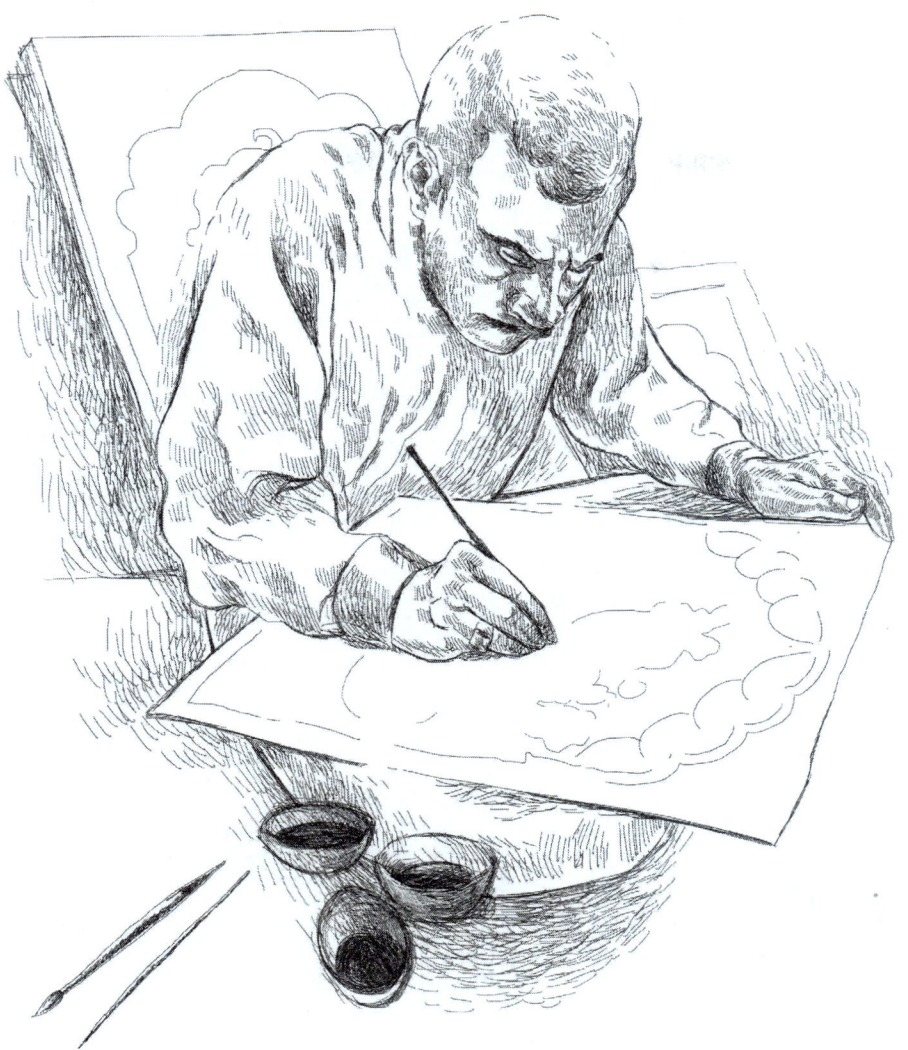

A Tanjore artist at work, face screwed up in concentration

The Tanjore Galaxy of Gods

Mainly intended for worship, Tanjore paintings—across eras and dynasties, be it the Cholas or the Marathas—were made as an alternative to idols, as you've already read. And so the themes too stayed religious, with Bal Gopal, or baby Lord Krishna, stealing balls of butter being the most common of all. Other Hindu gods like Shiva, Vishnu, Ganesha, Saraswati, Kartikeya and Annapurna were depicted too. So in earlier times, the knowledge of ancient scriptures was essential to creating Tanjore paintings.

The style and features too remained constant. These paintings had one primary subject—a chief deity who was at the centre of the painting, such as Lord Krishna, Rama or Goddess Lakshmi. And these central deities were accompanied by attendants or animals, like an elephant, horse or cow. The main subject was usually drawn bigger than the rest. There are paintings of baby Krishna, for example, in which he is shown as being even bigger than his mother Yashoda! As another feature of these paintings, sometimes only the main figure was painted and embellished with jewels, while the secondary subjects were done only as drawings.

Over the centuries, Tanjore art was influenced by various other religions as well, and today, you can find images of Buddhist and Jain deities, flying angels and even baby Krishna in the lap of Mother Mary! A superb example of the blending of different times and cultures, this!

The Elaborate Creation

Originally, the Tanjore artists used to prepare the paints using natural pigments. They created chubby-faced, round-bodied figures in luminous colours like red, blue and green and then drew

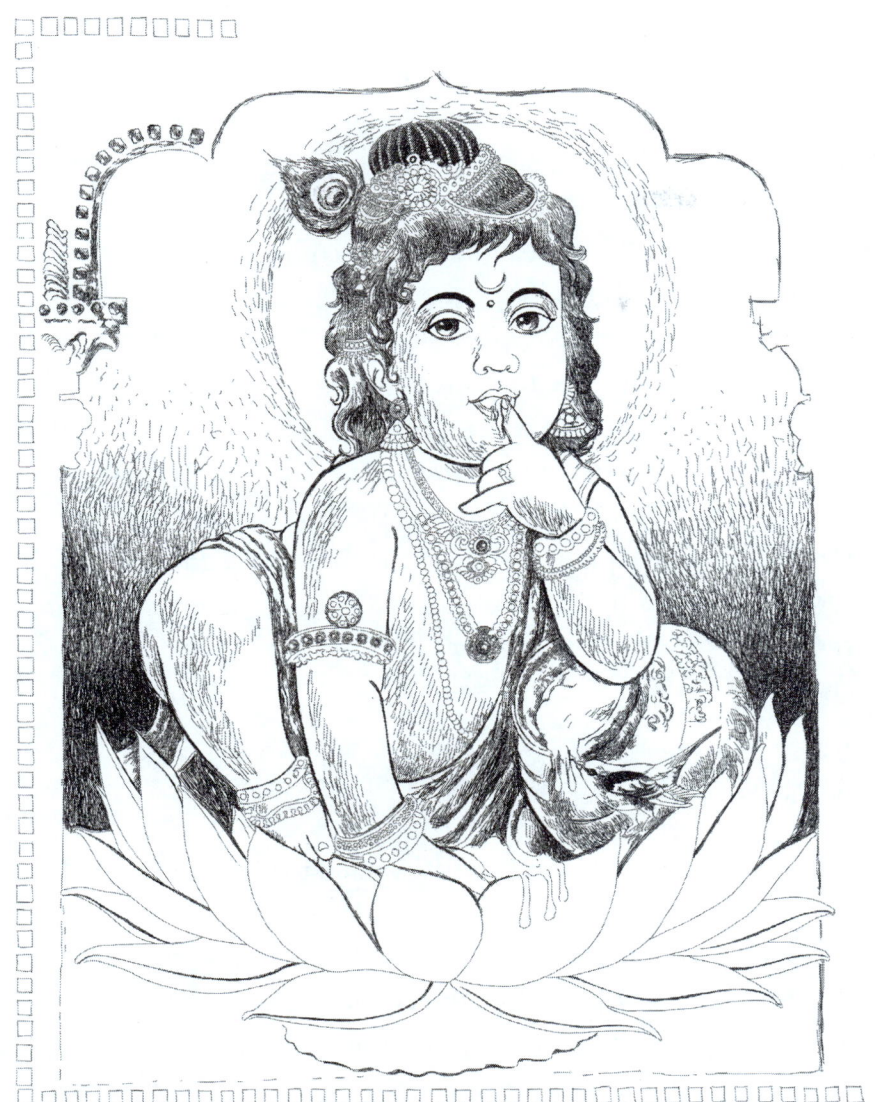

Bal Gopal sneaks some mouth-watering butter, as imagined in Tanjore art

the rich and luxurious ornamentation, comprising intricately drawn bolsters and cushions; flower garlands, such as delicate strings of lotus; jewellery, such as armlets, bangles, necklaces, toe-rings, finger-rings and even nose rings; and silken saris and dhotis with elaborate borders.

So, as you can guess, making a Tanjore painting was not easy. Even the smallest of these extravagant paintings takes about four to six months to complete. Imagine the meticulous process of pasting gold leaves and precious stones on walls and canvasses—how stressful, right? For a very long time, the original technique of making a Tanjore painting was kept a closely guarded secret by the artists. But as the years passed, due to the lack of royal interest and patronage, the artists had a tough time finding work and were forced to reveal their method. So what's this secret technique, you ask? Well, here it is in four simple steps: first, tamarind seed paste is applied on a cloth base; then it is coated with a paste made of limestone; after this, the cloth is fixed to a canvas, which is usually a plank fashioned from the jackfruit or teak tree (though many Tanjore artists use plywood these days); finally, once the surface is dry, the artist makes the sketch and colours it in, after which gems are inlaid in decorative patterns.

Sisters in Arms: The Story of Mysore Art

There's another style of painting that looks quite similar to the Tanjore style (you could easily confuse the two!) but is actually pretty different. This sibling art form is known as the Mysore style of painting. They're similar in that both Tanjore and Mysore paintings are created primarily for devotional purposes. But more importantly, both styles originated from the same source. Yep! Initially Tanjore art was mainly practised by two artist communities—the Rajus in Thanjavur and Trichy, and the Naidus in Madurai. But after the decline of the dynastic rule of the Vijayanagara Empire, some of the artists—primarily the Rajus—shifted to Mysore and started painting there. And a new style thus developed, which came to be known as the Mysore style.

Now for the differences: Well, for starters, the Mysore style is lesser known than its more famous counterpart, Tanjore. Plus, it's mostly done on paper and is less extravagant—usually gems are not used in Mysore paintings, and the focus is on a far more intricate method of drawing. Special ornamental frames with detailed designs and carvings are another feature of Mysore paintings.

A Recap: The Gilded Treasures

The tradition of the Tanjore style of painting goes back a very long time, and even today, artists try hard to stay true to the traditional practices, methods and themes. However, over a period of time, certain changes have crept into these paintings—the figures are no longer rounded or chubby; sometimes coloured glass is used instead of uncut gems; a number of deities are depicted in

Catch the Real Thing!

Government Museum, Chennai, and **Thanjavur Art Gallery and Museum**, Thanjavur, house fine collections of Tanjore paintings.

Where: Tamil Nadu

Entry:
- **Government Museum, Chennai:** Rs 15, Rs 10 and Rs 3 for adults, children and schoolchildren respectively (Indian nationals); Rs 250 for foreign nationals
- **Thanjavur Art Gallery and Museum:** Rs 10 and Rs 5 for adults and children respectively (Indian nationals); Rs 50 and Rs 25 for adults and children respectively (foreign nationals)

What to see: A gallery in the Government Museum has a superb collection of south Indian bronze sculptures.

Remember: Go on a weekday as the museums will be less crowded.

Know more at: www.chennaimuseum360.org; www.tanjore.net

the paintings rather than just one figure; and instead of temple and palace walls, the walls of hotels and offices (*how* times have changed!) are lined with these stunningly elaborate paintings. But even so, the Tanjore style of painting—with its exquisite detailing of jewellery, elaborate architectural features like arches and pillars, raised designs using gold foil that give it a sculptural quality and the highly refined skills required to put it all together—stands as a curious combination of architecture, sculpture, jewellery, painting and handicraft. You can even say it's a perfect mix of folk and classical forms of Indian art.

Keeping It Real

The Company School of Paintings and European Realism

Art Imitates Life

The British Conquest

For this art lesson, let's visit the time when India was under British rule in the eighteenth and nineteenth centuries. As you would know from your history classes, the East India Company, a powerful British trading firm, came to India to trade cotton, silk, spices and tea, but ended up colonizing the country. How is this possible, you wonder? Well, you know when you start with one little square of chocolate and then, bit by bit, before you know it, you've polished the entire thing off? That's exactly what happened here. Since the British arrived in India to trade, their commercial interests eventually sparked off a desire to rule the resource-rich country. They did this by establishing strong relationships with the local Indian kings to protect their own interests, and by playing one king against the other with pledges to help these maharajas overthrow their enemies (with their ever-growing private army) in return for special privileges. Soon they had these Indian kings under their control.

But not all Indian rulers were taken by this clever scheme of the British. The then nawab of Bengal, Siraj-ud-Daulah, saw through this wicked plan of divide and rule. So he began to shut down all British factories in Bengal. In order to stop him, Lord Robert Clive, a soldier and statesman in the East India Company, was sent to India to fight the famous Battle of Plassey against the nawab of Bengal in 1757. Unfortunately, the nawab lost—Clive had played the nawab by bribing his own army chief! And so the British established their rule here in Bengal and, over the next hundred years, helped themselves to the whole of India.

Artists and Co.

So how does art fit into all of this, you ask? Well, here's how . . . To rule and run a big country, the British needed many officials. And so, a great number of employees of the East India Company moved from England to India and started a new life in a new country. These people travelled through the subcontinent and discovered a way of life that was very different from theirs. They saw the stunning ancient monuments, people of diverse regions and the variety of flora and fauna. And they wanted to show these unusual things in their new home to their friends and relatives in England. Well, what better way to do so than capturing these images to send or take back to their homeland, right? (If only they had a camera, let alone Facebook or Instagram, in those days!) So the European officials and travellers hired Indian painters to do the job.

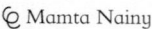

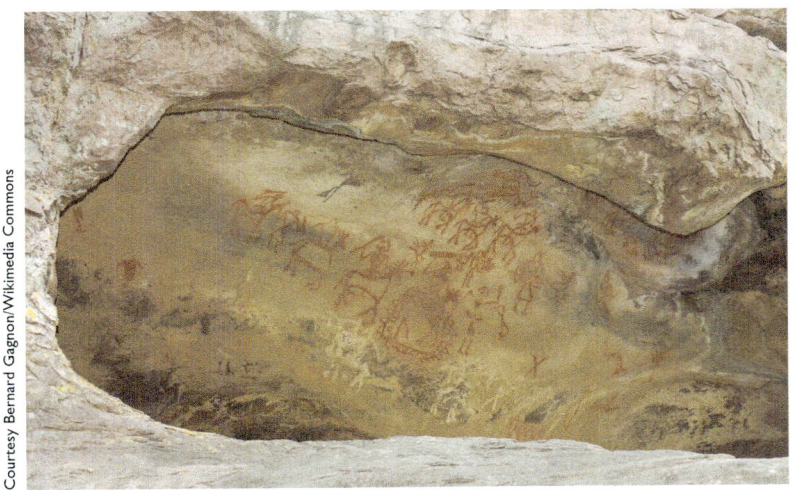

◀ This cave painting on the wall of Shelter 8 of the Bhimbetka Caves sure tells a story. Could it be a procession, or the artist's take on a conquest, perhaps?

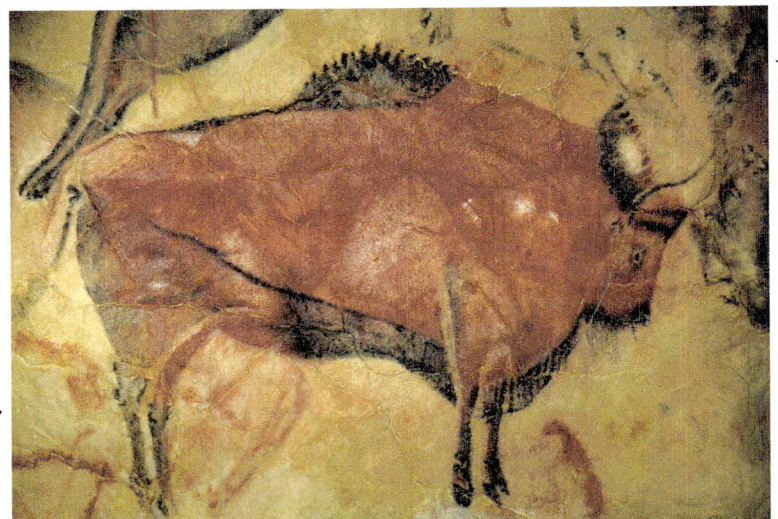

Oddly enough, it seems that early humans across ▶ the world had similar ideas about art. They covered their caves with artwork that recreated the world as they saw it—like this stunning bison that can be found in the Cave of Altamira in Spain.

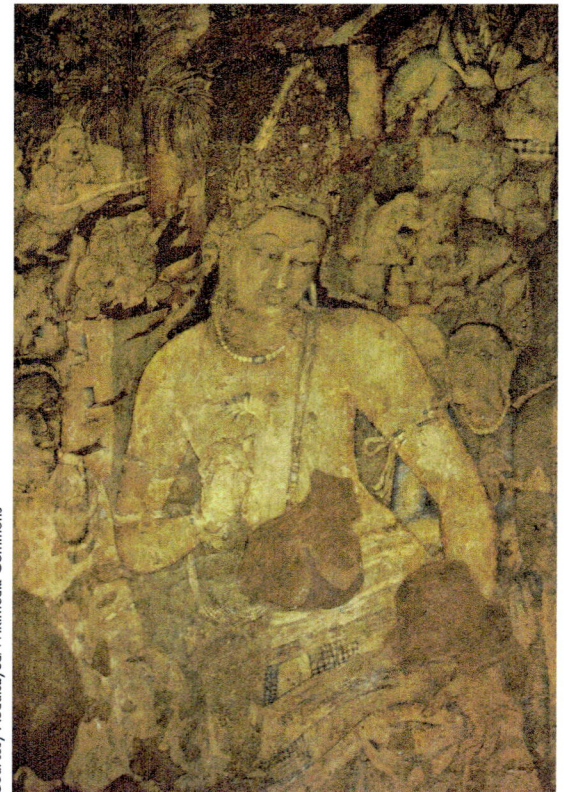

▲

The most famous of the Ajanta paintings depicts the bodhisattva Padmapani, or 'the one holding a lotus'. It's located to the left of an intricately carved door that leads to the Buddha's shrine in Cave 1. Depicted as a compassionate prince, the bodhisattva is shown here in a meditative state with his eyes half-closed. If you look carefully, you'll notice that the two arms of the bodhisattva look a bit awkward and long. This is because an ancient book on Indian sculpture suggests that great men are supposed to be portrayed with arms that look like elephant trunks!

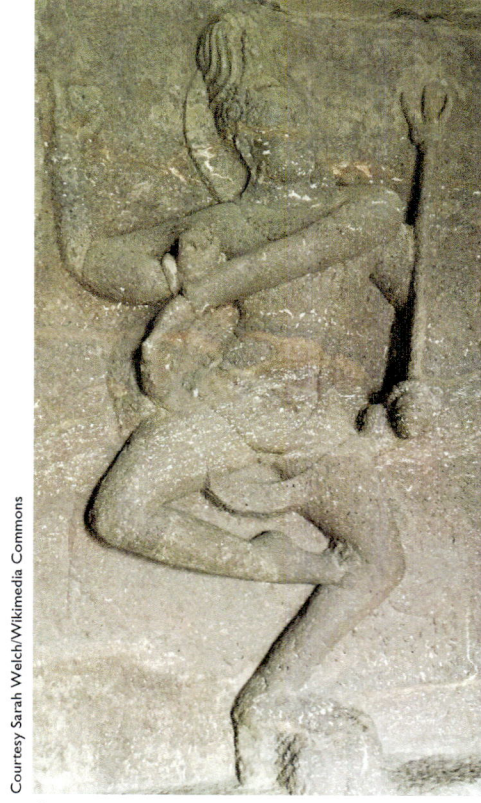

▲

Lord Shiva is depicted in sixty-four different poses in the Kailash Temple of Ellora. This is one of them—the Dancing Shiva.

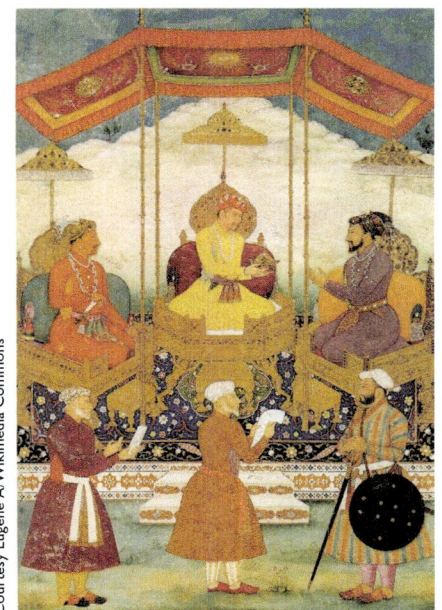

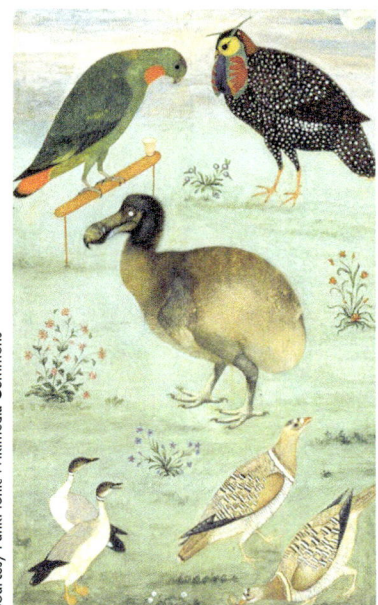

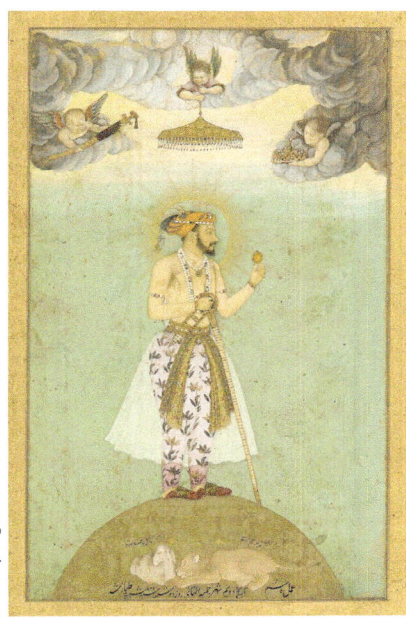

▲

This painting was done by a court artist called Bichitr, or 'the wondrous one', who was active during the reigns of Mughal emperors Jahangir and Shah Jahan. The work shows Emperor Akbar sitting in the centre and holding out his crown to his grandson Shah Jahan, instead of his son Jahangir. Bichitr portrays the conflict between father and son in this iconic painting.

▲

This painting of a dodo was created by Ustad Mansur during Jahangir's reign. It is believed that two live specimens of the dodo were specially brought to India during Jahangir's time.

▲

This Mughal miniature, made by a painter called Hashim, shows the emperor Shah Jahan standing on a globe. Can you spot a lion and a lamb sitting side by side inside the globe? This is a symbolic representation of the peaceful coexistence of living beings under Shah Jahan's rule.

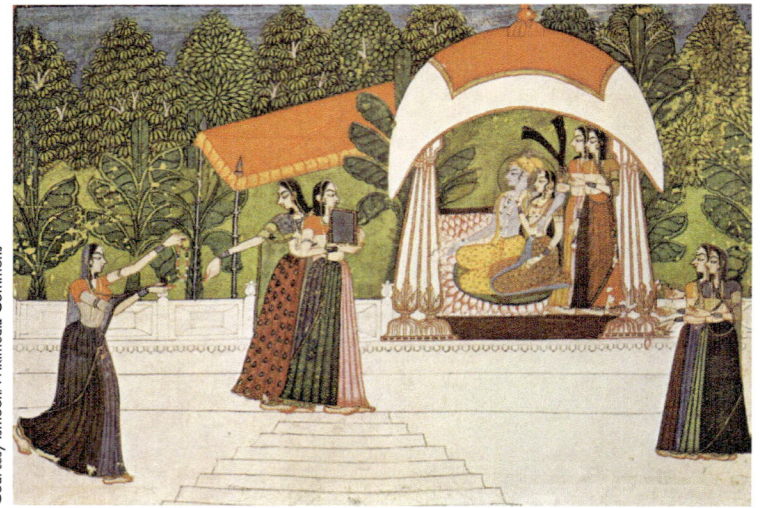

◀ This intricate and highly detailed Rajput miniature was made in the eighteenth century by Nihal Chand, the chief painter in the court of Kishangarh during the reign of Raja Sawant Singh. He is best known for his graceful depictions of Bani Thani.

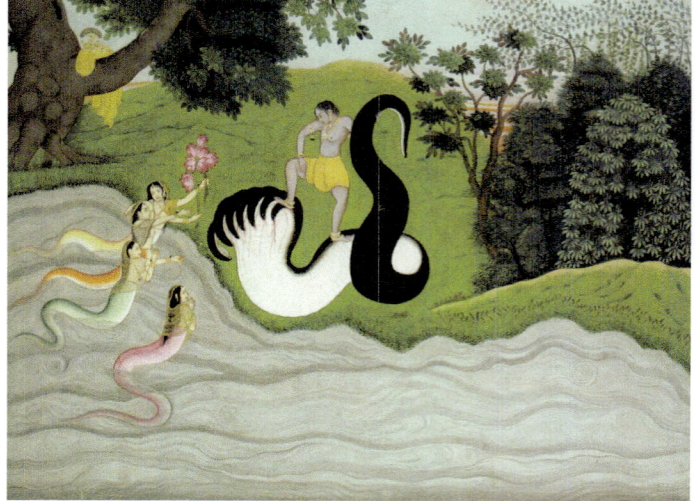

This Pahari (Kangra) miniature shows the wives of the ▶ great serpent Kaliya praying to Lord Krishna to release their husband. According to legend, Kaliya poisoned the waters of River Yamuna, after which Lord Krishna defeated him in a duel, leapt on to his hood and danced on it.

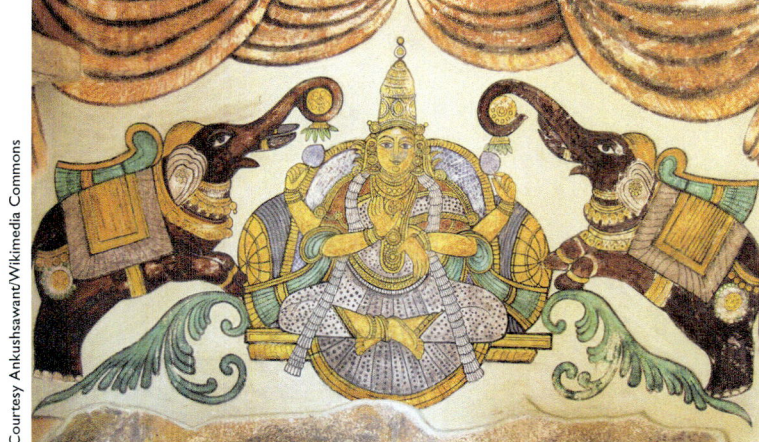

A wall painting in Thanjavur's Brihadeeshwara Temple, from where Tanjore paintings are said to have originated

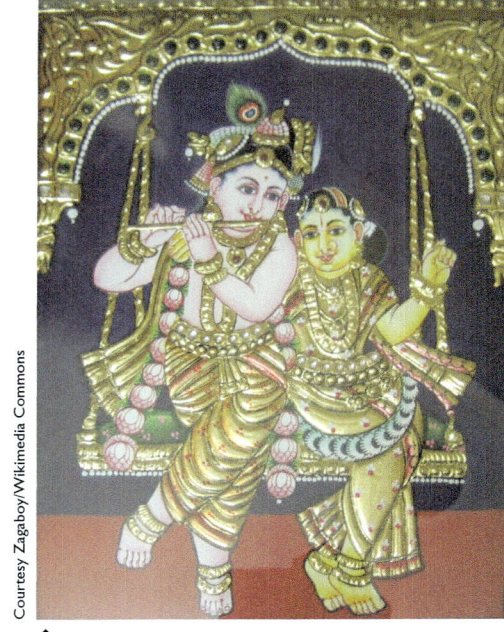

A Tanjore painting—complete with details in gold foil—of Lord Krishna and his wife Queen Rukmini sitting on a golden swing

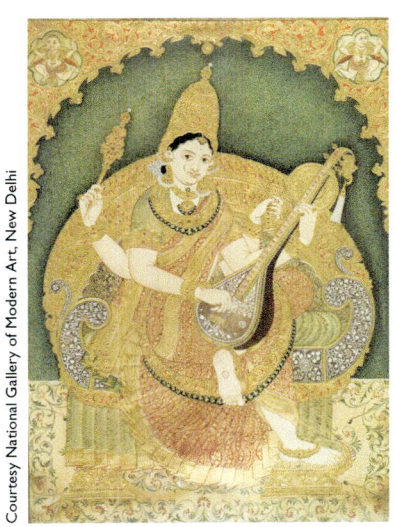

◀ An example of the understated cousin of Tanjore paintings—Mysore paintings—depicting Goddess Saraswati sitting on an elaborate throne

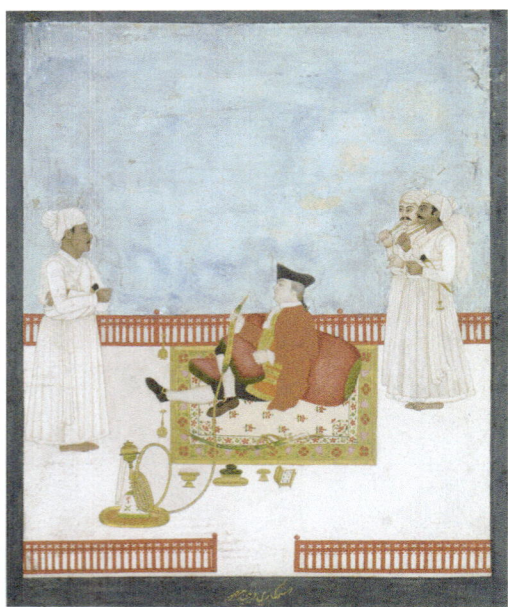

◀ A fine example of the Company school of art, this painting—by Indian painter Dip Chand—shows the British official William Fullerton of Rosemount, who became the mayor of Calcutta in 1757.

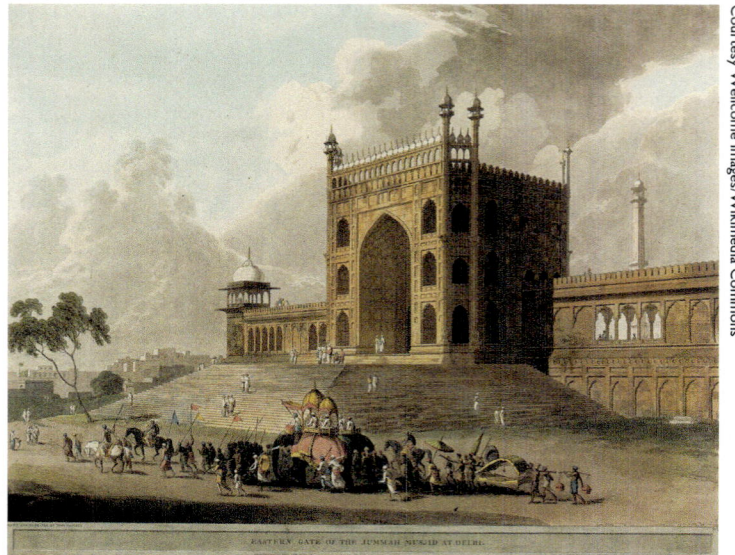

British landscape artist Thomas Daniell's painting ▶ of the Jama Masjid, or the Jummah Musjid, in Shahjahanabad (Old Delhi)

◀ The British opened art schools in India to train Indian artists in the Western style of painting, which was realistic. This painting, titled *At Rest*, is by one such Indian artist, who studied at Sir J.J. School of Art in Bombay—Pestonjee Bomanjee.

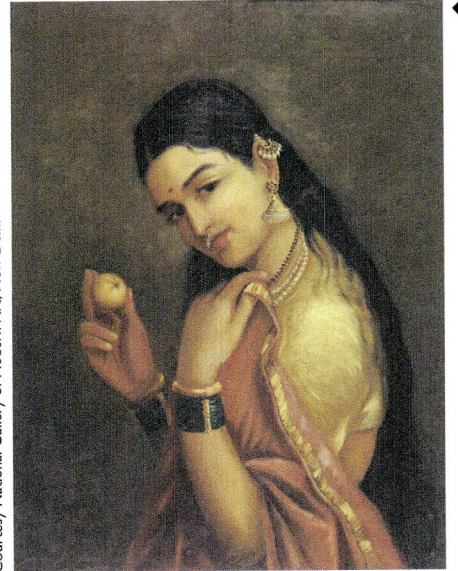

◀ A stunning, lifelike painting of a woman wearing intricately detailed jewellery and holding a fruit, by the famous painter prince of India, Raja Ravi Varma

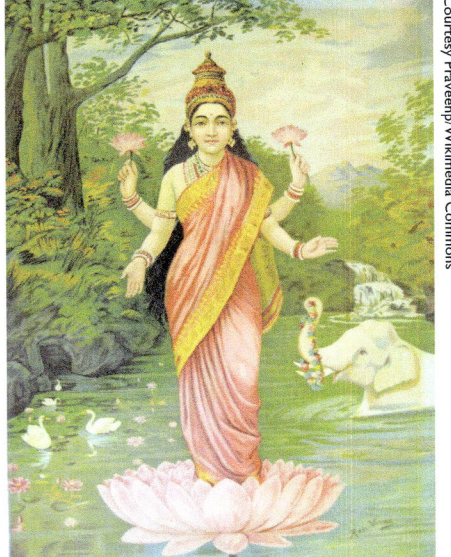

An oleograph of Goddess ▶
Lakshmi by Raja Ravi Varma

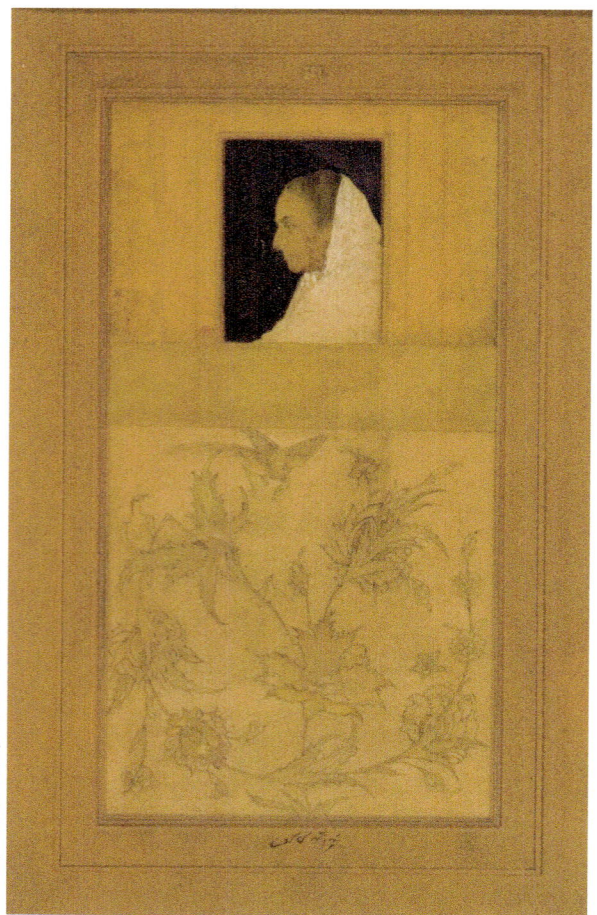

◀ This painting, titled *My Mother*, was made by the pioneer of the Bengal school of art, Abanindranath Tagore. After his mother's death, Abanindranath realized that there was neither a photograph nor a portrait of her. So he painted her image in profile, similar to a miniature painting.

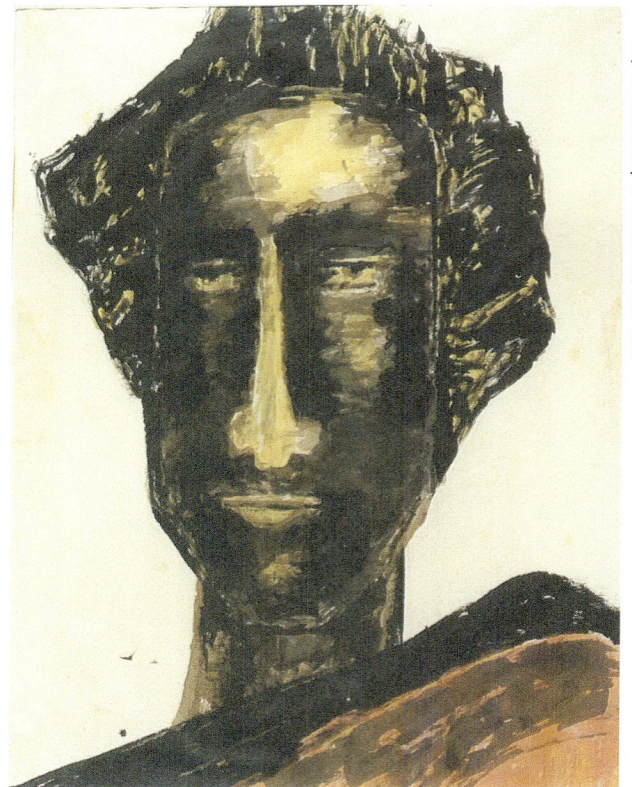

Rabindranath Tagore, who started painting quite late in life, ▶ created some highly imaginative and spontaneous works, like this head study on a silk cloth!

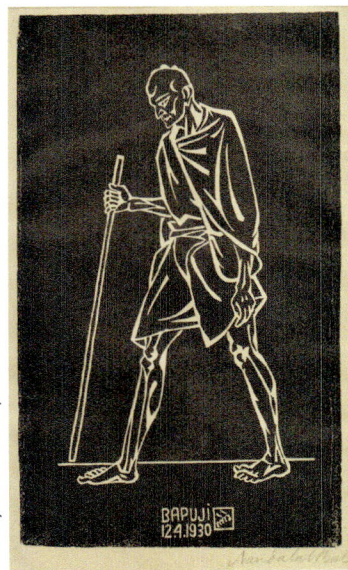

◀ Nandalal Bose had a close relationship with Mahatma Gandhi. This black-and-white print titled *Bapuji* was done by the artist in 1930 to commemorate the Dandi March.

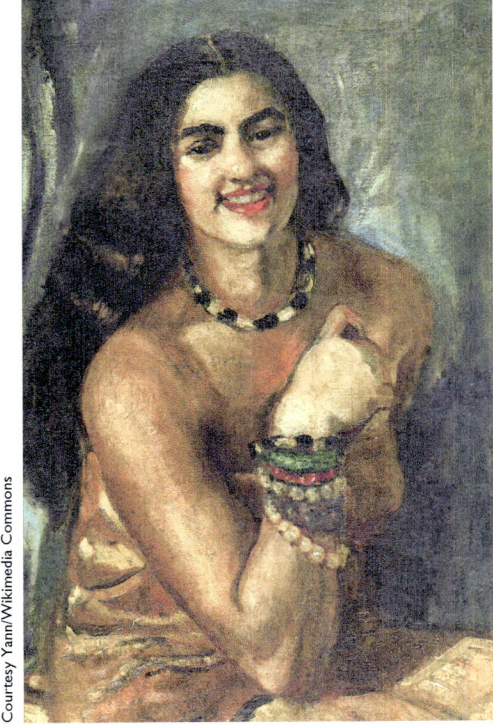

▲ A self-portrait of Amrita Sher-Gil. But how does one draw oneself? Easy-peasy! By sitting in front of a mirror!

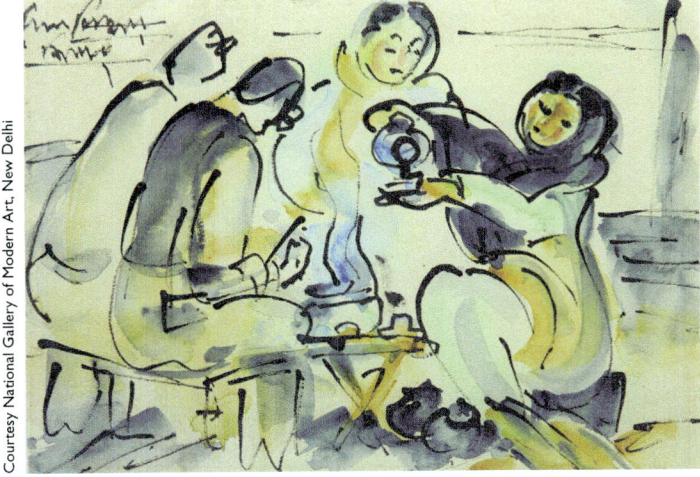

◀ A painting of a tea shop by the experimental painter and sculptor Ramkinkar Baij

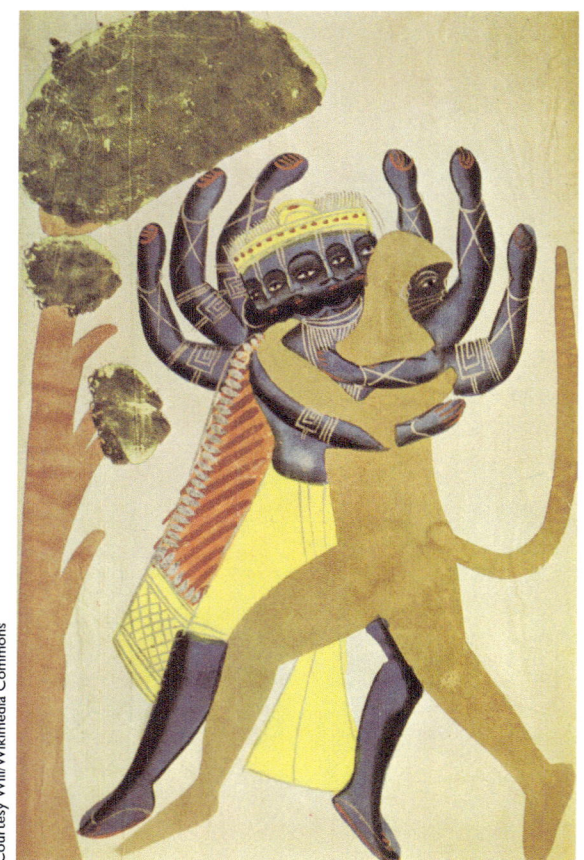

A Kalighat painting of the blue-skinned, multi-headed demon king of Lanka, Ravana, fighting Hanuman, the monkey god

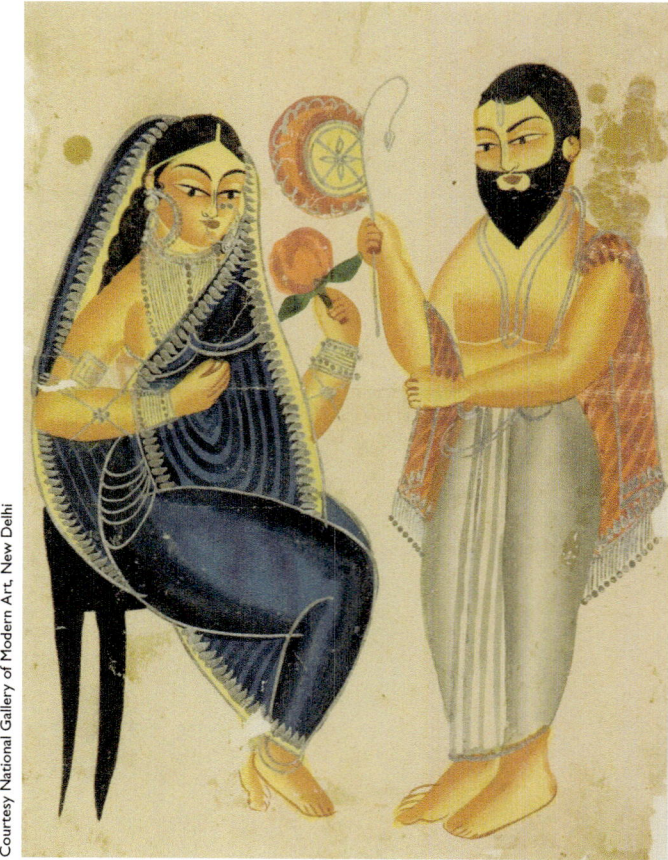

Made in 1880, this Kalighat painting depicts a very famous public scandal, wherein a priest, Mahant, is shown fanning Elokeshi, the attractive young wife of a clerk.

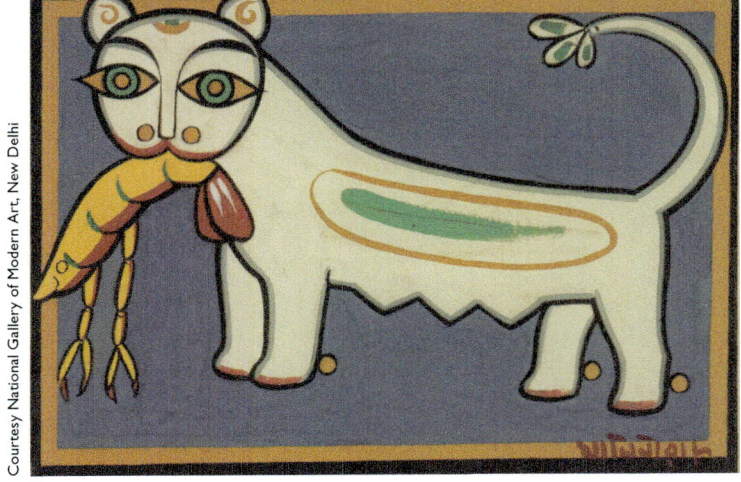

◀ A cat with a lobster was a popular theme in Kalighat paintings, wherein the cat was representative of greedy priests. In this work, Jamini Roy further simplified the figure of the cat with his bold and charming style.

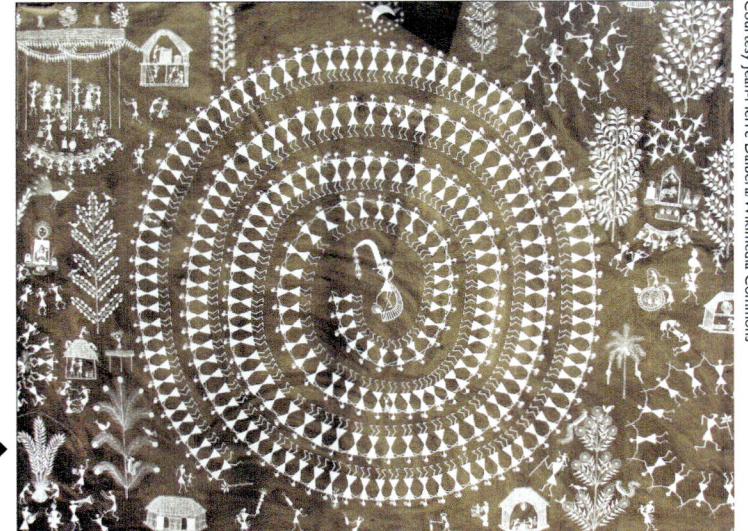

An impressive Warli painting by Jivya Soma Mashe, ▶ who contributed a great deal to popularizing this folk art form. Can you spot all the different activities that the figures are up to in this painting?

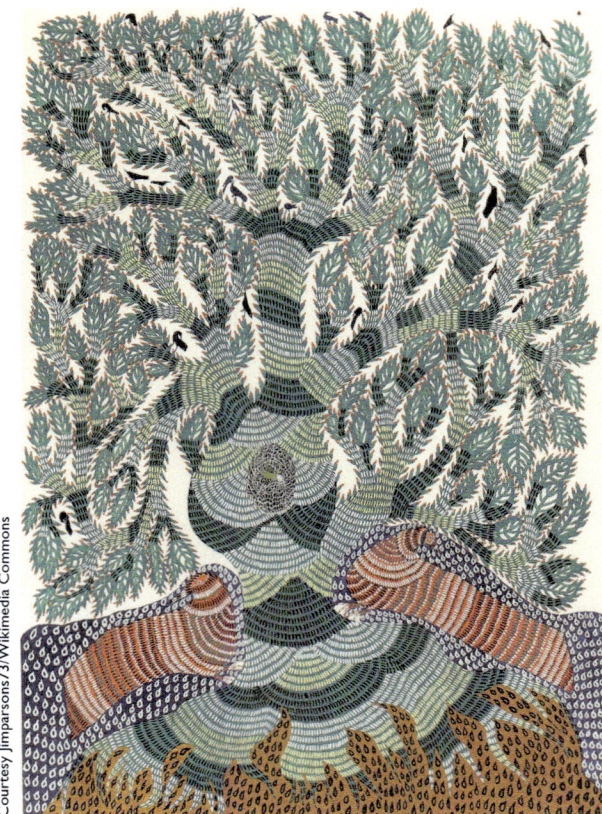

A famous Gond painting by artist Jangarh Singh Shyam done in unique patterns. He was one of the first Gond artists to use paper for his paintings. Here's a test: can you spot a spider in this beautiful artwork?

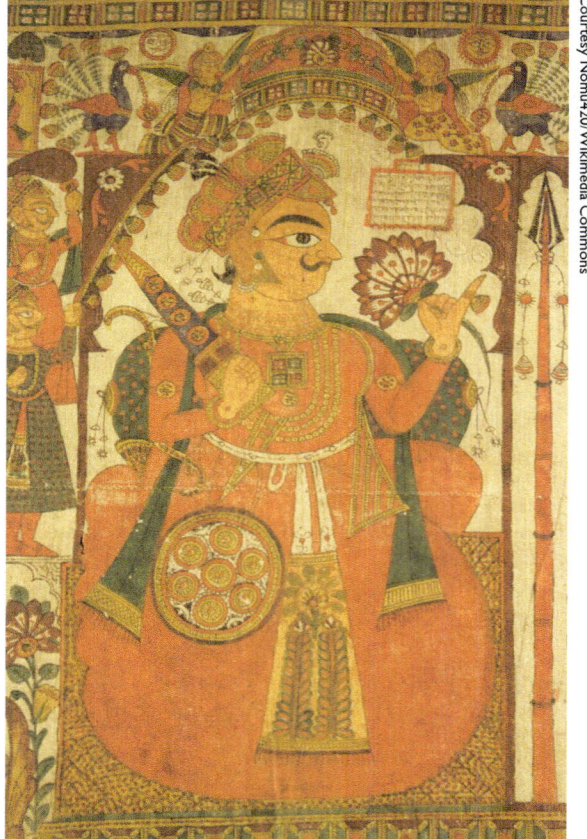

Notice the details in this Phad painting, a unique art form practised in Rajasthan. This phad depicts the life and adventures of the local folk hero Pabuji.

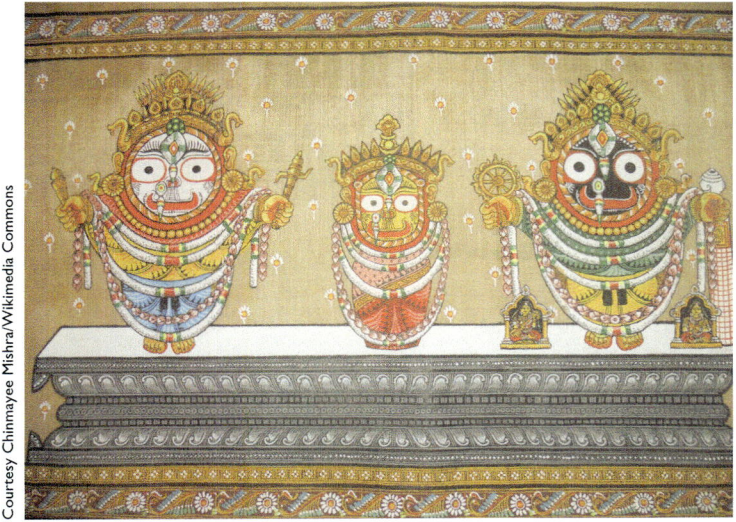

◀ An Odisha pat painting of Jagannath, Balarama and Subhadra, using the three main colours—white, yellow and black—for the different gods

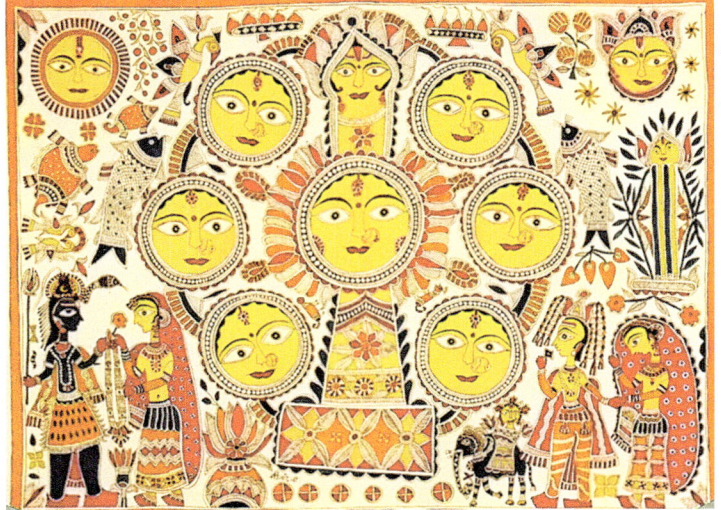

It is believed that the first Mithila paintings were done ▶ to decorate the palace walls on the occasion of Rama and Sita's wedding. Even today, the walls of a bride and groom's wedding chamber (*kohbar ghar*) are decorated with Mithila paintings known as Kohbar. This extraordinary Kohbar is by the famous Mithila painter Sita Devi.

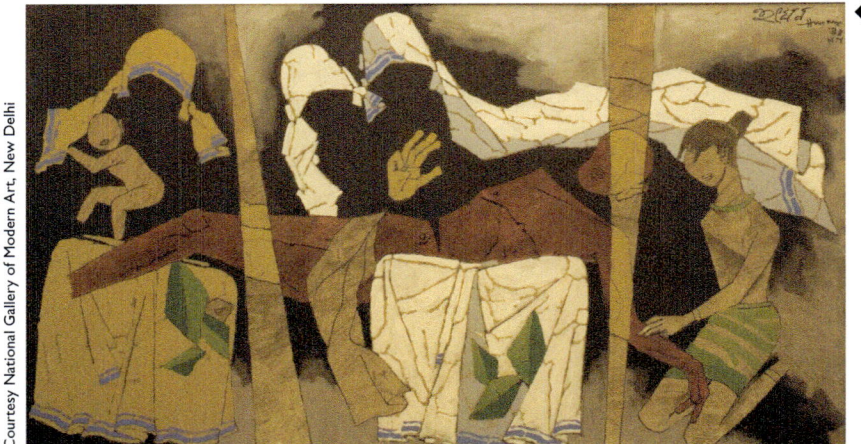

◀ Do you recognize this well-known painting from somewhere? The faceless rendering of Mother Teresa in her iconic white sari with a blue border was painted by the foremost modern Indian artist—Maqbool Fida Husain. What do you think is the concept behind this painting?

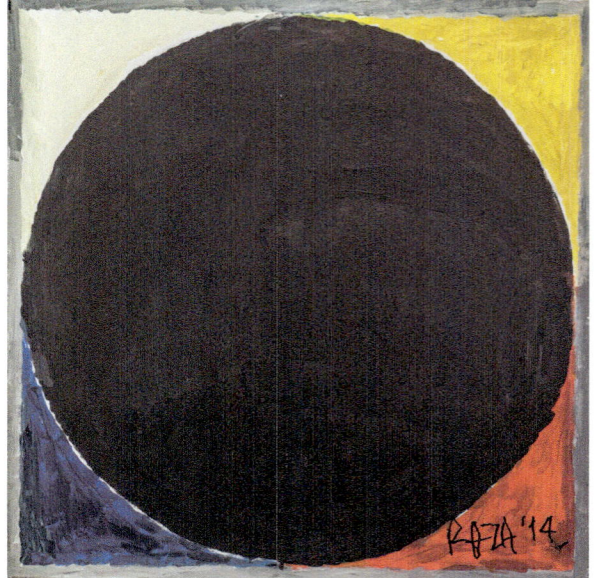

When Sayed Haider Raza was looking to rediscover himself ▶ through his paintings, the bindu, or dot, came to his rescue. The bindu in this painting is in the form of the *panch tatva*, or the 'five elements' (earth, water, air, space and fire). It is believed that everything—even human beings—is made of these five elements.

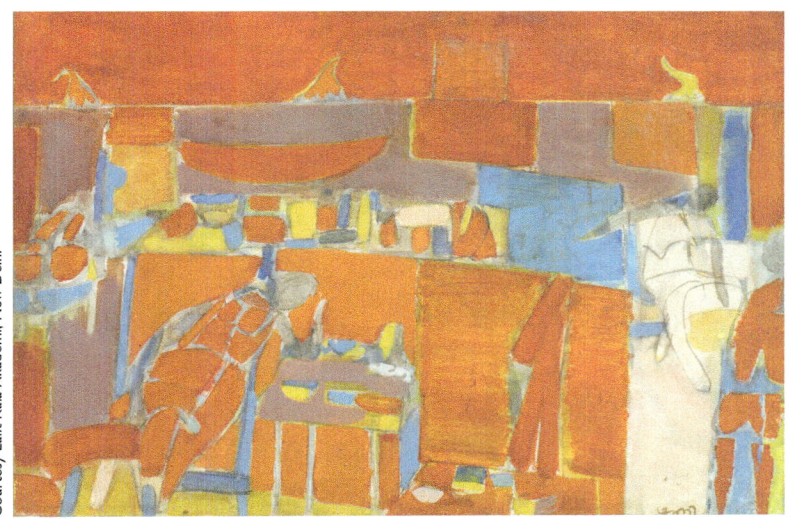

◀ A modern artwork titled *Studio* by one of India's most renowned artists, K.G. Subramanyan, who taught at the faculty of fine arts, Maharaja Sayajirao University of Baroda, and later at Kala Bhavana in Santiniketan

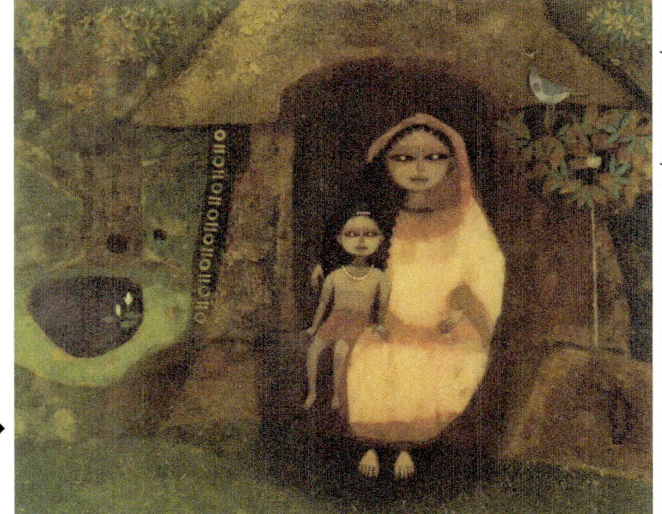

A painting of a mother and child sitting in front of their hut ▶ by Ganesh Pyne. Doesn't the child look like a young Lord Krishna, and the mother, like Goddess Durga? Do they look a little scared to you? But what are they scared of?

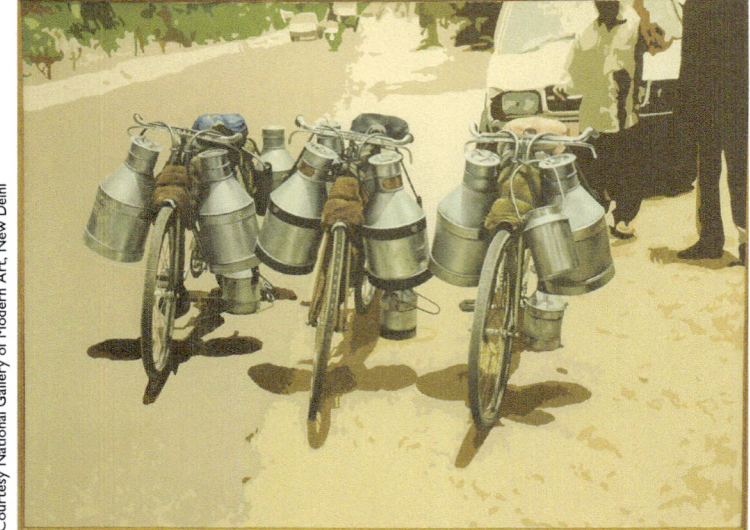

◀ A famous piece by the contemporary artist Subodh Gupta, called *Three Cows*. Why is it named so? Because in towns and cities, milk comes in big cans that hang from bicycles, in contrast to cows being directly milked by folks in villages!

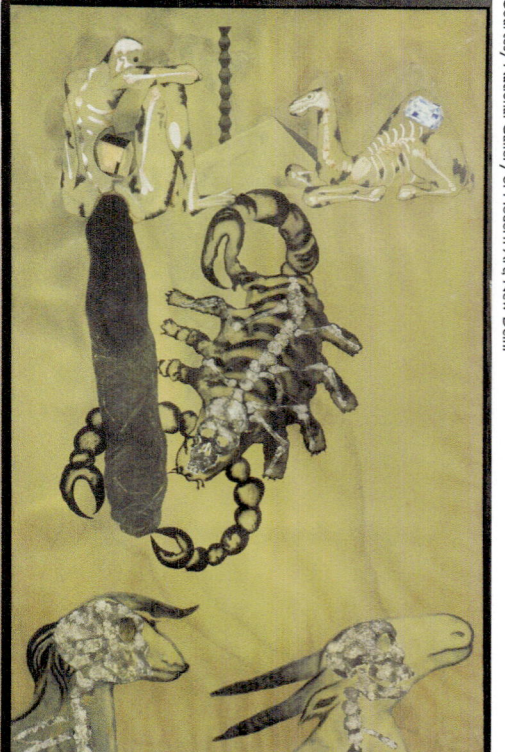

Titled *Desert Halt*, this painting by contemporary artist ▶ Atul Dodiya depicts the crisis of the modern world. What do you feel when you look at this work?

These painters were often those who had been previously employed at the Mughal courts. (If you came in late, or have been trying to read the book from back to front, you can go to the chapter on Mughal art and read all about it there.) Since the Mughal Empire was well past its prime, and the artists were finding it difficult to survive without patronage, they started offering their services to the British officials and created the kind of paintings the new patrons wanted. The paintings thus made, to satisfy the curiosity of the British people in England about the colonies and their natives, came to be known as—guess what? The Company school of paintings, for they were done during the time of the East India Company.

The Company school first emerged in the town of Murshidabad in West Bengal and later spread to other centres such as Delhi, Lucknow, Tanjore, Benares (present-day Varanasi) and Trichinopoly (present-day Tiruchirappalli). However, towards the end of the eighteenth century, many artists from Murshidabad moved to Patna (the present-day capital of Bihar) and the city became the headquarters of this style of painting. Hence the Company school of paintings is also known as the Patna school of paintings.

The Tight Grip of Realism

The British had different aesthetics with regard to art, and the Indian artists knew that if they were to survive, they'd have to start understanding and painting from the British point of view. Hence, the artists moved to a more realistic sort of painting style, which meant that they tried to draw exactly what they saw, for these paintings were as much for documentation purposes as they were for artistic ones. They tried adapting to the ways of the British, and what came out of that was a mix of Indian and European art styles. Not surprisingly, the painters used familiar techniques from the Mughal paintings and then joined them with the features of a Western style of painting.

The Company paintings did not use natural colours, as now colours were not organically created from minerals and rocks like they were during the Mughal period, but were done in watercolours. (You know what that means, don't you? The paints that you use today came from this era!) The Indian artists also started training themselves with new materials, such as pen and ink, and in new techniques, like shading, so that their paintings appealed to the British. Regardless of the new styles and methods, these paintings tended to have fairly usual subjects, like animals and birds, landscapes and the Indian way of life.

Snapshots of History

Some British civil servants in India started collecting the paintings they commissioned out to Indian artists into albums.

The Fraser Album, commissioned by William and James Fraser from 1815 to 1819, is one such album, which holds more than ninety coloured pictures on a wide variety of Indian subjects.

The Delhi Book, or *Reminiscences of Imperial Delhie*, which has about 120 paintings commissioned by Sir Thomas Metcalfe in 1844, is another fine example of these albums.

During this period, some artists from Britain and other European countries too came here; they also saw a lucrative opportunity in this rich and vibrant land. Among them were about thirty British portrait artists, who came to India in search of work and were trained in a technique called oil painting. They travelled the length and breadth of the country and made a large number of paintings. Some of these artists were William Hodges, Johan Zoffany and the uncle–nephew duo Thomas and William Daniell. These travelling artists created astonishingly realistic oil paintings on big canvasses that looked just like photographs. They painted India as an exotic, mysterious land, with vivid depictions of the ghats of Benares, girls dancing in the courts, colourful costumes, beautiful landscapes, different native occupations, etc.

However, with time, these foreign artists found that painting portraits was far more lucrative than landscapes and other drawings. So they started making authorized portraits of high-ranking British officials and the elite, which were hung in public buildings like the town hall and government offices. The price of these portraits depended on how popular the painter was. So while a renowned painter charged about 120 gold mohurs or coins for a single portrait, a not-so-famous painter made some forty gold coins for a similar work. But these painters truly did a good job with the portraits—when viewing their works, you feel as though you're sitting face-to-face with the real person. No detail was missed—the wrinkles, receding hairlines, sagging jowls and even the paunches of some of the British officers are captured vividly in these paintings!

The Birth of Art Schools in India

Thus, in the late nineteenth century, with the arrival of the European painters and with Indian painters being exposed to and adapting to European styles of painting, came about a major swing in public taste. Lifelike paintings done in an extremely realistic fashion suddenly became very popular. And to promote the European style of painting further, the British opened several art schools in India, like Government School of Art in Calcutta (present-day Kolkata) and Sir J.J. School of Art in Bombay (present-day Mumbai). Here they admitted Indian students from educated, well-to-do backgrounds and trained them in fine art. They taught their students how to paint objects realistically and schooled them in new mediums, such as oil paints. This is how a whole new generation of Indian painters was born, trained in this novel style of realism that was learnt from the

British in Bombay and Calcutta. Some of these artists were Pestonjee Bomanjee, M.F. Pithawalla, Hemendranath Majumdar and Antonio Xavier Trindade.

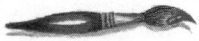

Raja Ravi Varma: The Life and Times

The Genius Painter from the South

While some painters were being trained by the British in Calcutta and Bombay, a most remarkable artist was born in south India, in the region of Trivandrum, Kerala. Do you know who this artist was? No? Okay, close your eyes and think of an image of a Hindu god or goddess. Done? Now, chances are that what you just imagined has been influenced by the work of this artist. Yes, most of the pictures of Hindu gods, goddesses and other characters from Indian classics that we see today in calendars, on TV and even in comics are based on the paintings of this one great Indian artist. His name? Raja Ravi Varma.

Ravi Varma was born in the village of Kilimanoor, a small estate in the kingdom of Travancore (present-day Thiruvananthapuram) in Kerala. As a little boy, Varma could be found doodling on the walls of his home or the neighbourhood temple. His uncle, who was himself a Tanjore artist, recognized Varma's budding talent and gave him basic lessons in art. When Varma was fourteen, his uncle helped him attain the patronage of the maharaja of Travancore. There the little boy studied different Indian and Western styles of painting and also learnt watercolours from the palace painter.

The Hush-Hush Education of Ravi Varma

One day, Ravi Varma saw a newspaper advertisement for oil paints. He really wanted to try out this new medium. So he ordered the oil colours from Madras. Oil colours obtained, his next dilemma was how to paint with these colours. It was yet an unfamiliar medium in India and not many knew how to use it. Only one person in the whole of Travancore knew the technique of painting in oil colours—the palace painter Ramaswamy Naicker. But Naicker saw a rival in young Varma and refused to train him. One of Naicker's students, though, Arumugham Pillai, felt really bad for the boy and decided to help him. How? He would sneak into the palace at night to teach Varma oil painting!

Ravi Varma also learnt this new medium by observing the Dutch portrait painter Theodor Janson, who was visiting the royal court of Travancore at that time to paint the portraits of the maharaja and his wife. Thus, with trial and error and hard work, Ravi Varma mastered this art even though he had no proper training.

The Student Schools the Teacher

When Raja Ravi Varma learnt to paint in oil colours, he too tried his hand at the portraits of the royal couple of the kingdom of Travancore. And his talent far surpassed the Dutchman!

When the Gods Went Glamorous

Once Ravi Varma became well versed in the art of painting in oil colours, he started drawing scenes from the Ramayana and the Mahabharata. His paintings of various episodes from these epics, such as Sita longing for the golden deer, the demon king Ravana abducting Sita, Yashoda holding an infant Krishna, are considered masterpieces. Using oil paints, he was able to create the most realistic representations of the characters in Indian epics and scriptures.

Varma was also greatly influenced by the dance forms of Kathakali and Koodiyattam, which he grew up watching in Kerala. Perhaps that is the reason his paintings were also composed like scenes from a dance drama. Set against beautifully detailed and ornate backgrounds, such as lush landscapes or splendid interior spaces, the characters in his paintings stood out perfectly in their elaborate jewellery and clothes, against glossy foliage or fine curtains. This style—of drapery and intricate scenes in the backdrop—created a sense of distance and depth in his paintings. It also made things appear three-dimensional. Just picture a painting in which the characters appear like stage actors standing in front of gorgeous sets!

Ravi Varma was also well known for his mastery over facial expressions. He carefully selected emotive legends from Indian classics and famously highlighted the feminine expression most vividly in his paintings. Adorned in delicate brocade saris and glittering jewels, the nayikas, or heroines, in his paintings, such as Shakuntala, Damayanti, Subhadra and Sita, became classic examples of Indian beauty.

With time, Raja Ravi Varma also became an accomplished portrait artist. His fame soared when he was asked to make several portraits of the Indian aristocracy and British officials. In fact, so popular did he become that the town of Kilimanoor had to specially open a post office for

Ravi Varma Becomes a 'Raja'

In 1873, Ravi Varma won the first prize at an art exhibition in Vienna and became a celebrated artist worldwide. Varma did not belong to the royal family of Travancore, and was therefore not a raja. But when the Vienna award was conferred on him, the title of raja was prefixed to Varma's name, and it stayed on forever.

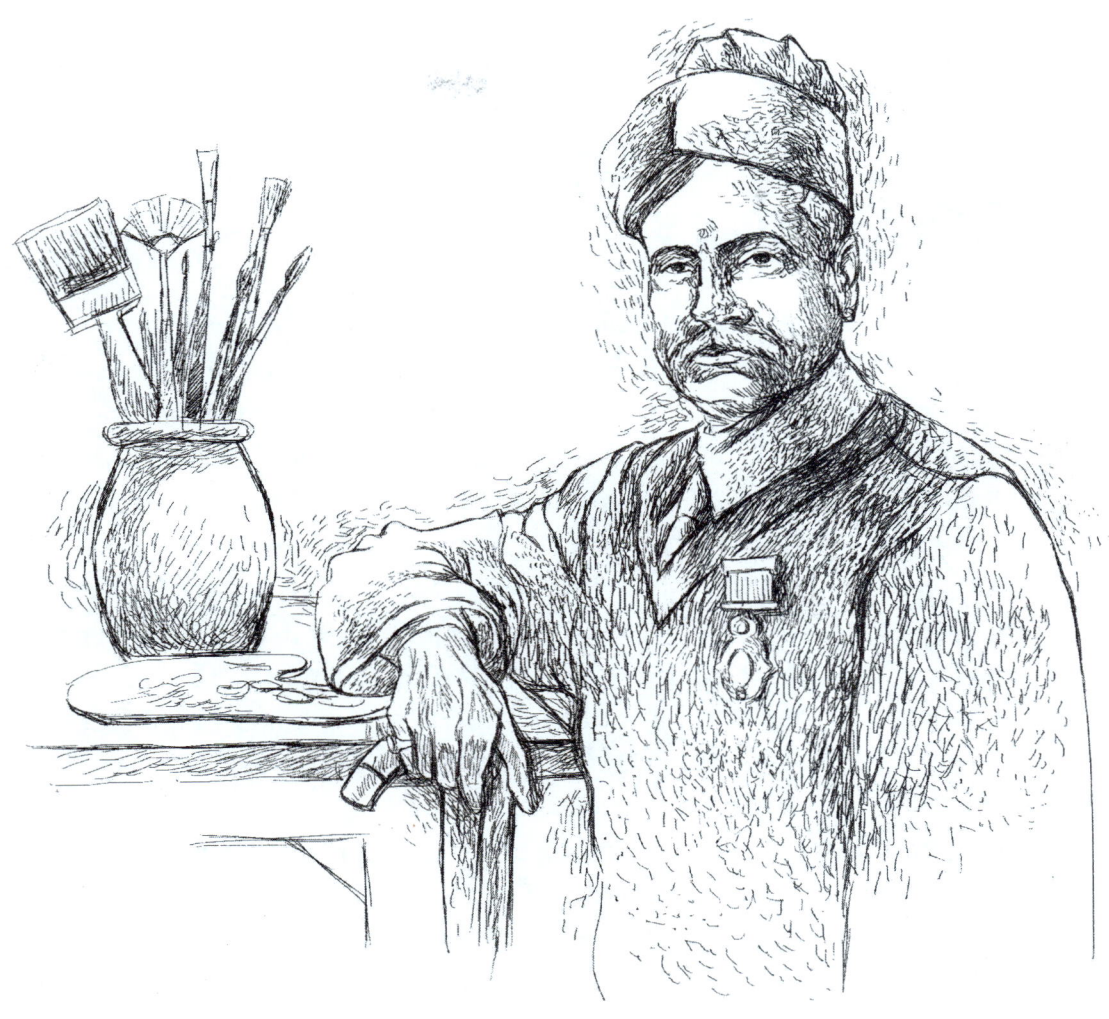

Raja Ravi Varma, who even mastered the self-portrait

the many letters that started arriving for Varma from every corner of the country, requesting him for portrait paintings!

Oleographs: Art for the Masses

Raja Ravi Varma had a grand vision. He wanted his paintings to reach a large number of people and at a price that ordinary people could afford. So he decided to make prints of his paintings. What an ingenious idea, isn't it? These prints were called oleographs. Varma first got these prints made in Germany in the early 1890s and then, in 1894, he started his own press in Bombay. Soon, people were buying the oleographs, and they even started worshipping Varma's paintings of gods and goddesses. Ravi Varma had made it big indeed!

But you didn't forget that all this was happening against the backdrop of the British Raj, did you? At the turn of the twentieth century, the struggle for India's independence gained momentum and patriotism swept the country. And Ravi Varma's paintings even became a symbol of patriotism, for they depicted subjects from Indian mythology. Varma's art became so well known and loved by the Indian people that they came to be used in labels and advertisements of many products—right from baby food to tinned sweets to calendars to matchboxes! People even started making unusual collages by pasting cut-outs of different characters against the scenic and elaborate backgrounds of Ravi Varma's paintings. There are pictures, for instance, in which the image of Mahatma Gandhi is superimposed on prints of Ravi Varma's painting of Lord Rama—to depict that Gandhi had the blessings of Lord Rama himself! It is because of this popular quality and wide circulation of his prints that Ravi Varma's works came to be known as calendar art or bazaar art.

A Recap: A Matter of Opinion

By now you know that Raja Ravi Varma was single-handedly responsible for bringing about a unique turn in the Indian art sphere during this period. His paintings shaped the very way Indians imagined gods and goddesses. And even after so many years, you will notice that his representations of these gods and goddesses still adorn our homes. Because of his influence and unique style—that combined Western painting techniques and Indian sensibilities—there was a spurt of mass interest in art in India.

However, like all famous painters, this artist too has had his share of disapproval from people. Some argue that Varma's work is too showy and is 'Indian' only on the surface, for it imitates the Western style of realism and uses oil as a medium of painting. The artist is also criticized for making gods appear more human and for presenting a very cosmetic or superficial view of art as well as mythology, which simply fails to stir any real emotion in the onlooker. Is that actually true? you might ask. Well, you review his paintings and be the judge.

Catch the Real Thing!

Government Museum, Chennai, and **National Gallery of Modern Art (NGMA), New Delhi**, have impressive collections of Ravi Varma's paintings and prints.

Where: Tamil Nadu and Delhi

Entry:
- **Government Museum, Chennai:** Rs 15, Rs 10 and Rs 3 for adults, children and schoolchildren respectively (Indian nationals); Rs 250 for foreign nationals
- NGMA: Rs 20 for Indian nationals; free admission for children below eighteen years of age; Rs 500 for foreign nationals

What to see: Just walk around and soak in the beauty of the Ravi Varma pieces!

Remember: The NGMA also houses an unmissable collection of Company paintings. What an added bonus!

Know more at: www.chennaimuseum360.org; www.ngmaindia.gov.in

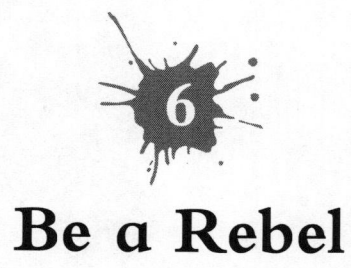

Be a Rebel

The Bengal School of Art

Home Is Where the Art Is

Imagine this: One day, some people come marching into your house, that you've been living in all your life, and tell you that they've come to take it over. What will you do?

A. You will politely ask them to leave. But what if they don't pay heed to your request?

B. You will try to throw them out. But what if they prove to be more powerful than you?

C. You will continue to protest . . . in whatever way you can. You won't want to give up your loving home, will you?

If you choose option C after trying options A and B, you will do the exact same thing that our forefathers did under British rule! As your history books must have taught you, after the British colonized India under the guise of trade, Indians tried everything in their power to get the British out of the country and become a free people. There was a major uprising in 1857; many talks were held between the two sides, during which the Indian people tried to put their point across; and violent revolts broke out too. But nothing seemed to work. So at the beginning of the twentieth century, the people of India decided to take up non-violent means of resistance, later championed by Mahatma Gandhi. One of these involved Indians boycotting British products, for which India was one of the biggest markets. They rejected everything videshi, or foreign, by burning British-made goods and opting for swadeshi items, or those goods that were manufactured in the country. Indians started wearing local hand-spun and handwoven clothes, rather than the clothes produced in British factories. This came to be known as the Swadeshi movement. And as the feeling of patriotism—of going back to everything Indian—swept through the country, it found its way into Indian art too.

Patriotism on the Palette

During the mid-nineteenth century, the British had opened many art schools in the country, which taught and promoted the Western way of painting. Thus it gained widespread admiration in India, so much so that Indian artists even tried hard to copy the Western style! (Did you read the earlier chapter on Company paintings, European traveller artists and Raja Ravi Varma?) Therefore, oil on canvas, and a realistic and lifelike method of painting was considered the *only* way of painting by now.

It was during this time, with the rise of patriotism and the rapid growth of the Independence movement, that a group of Indian painters tried to regain an 'Indian' identity and independence in art. They realized that copying Western styles wasn't the way forward. They searched for their forgotten cultural heritage and the 'Indian' way of painting by looking at India's rich past and not the British. This art movement started mainly in Calcutta and Santiniketan in Bengal and thus came to be known as the Bengal school of art.

Abanindranath: The Visionary Tagore

Though the British were in India as colonizers, there were some officials who helped Indian artists find their artistic identity. Like the British reformer E.B. Havell. He was the principal of Government School of Art, Calcutta, and encouraged his students to look at Mughal miniatures and other traditional Indian art forms for inspiration instead of suggesting they blindly copy Western art.

A Man of Many Talents

Just like his uncle Rabindranath Tagore, Abanindranath Tagore was also a writer. He has a number of children's books to his name.

He was supported by painter and writer Abanindranath Tagore, who was the vice-principal of Government School of Art at that time. You might recognize the surname Tagore . . . Does it ring a bell? Well, Abanindranath was the nephew of the famous writer and painter Rabindranath Tagore! An artist himself, Abanindranath consciously avoided the use of oil colours. He opposed the British style of painting by using art supplies that were available locally—the ones used in traditional Indian paintings like those of Ajanta and the Mughal miniatures. The subjects he painted were also very Indian—mostly inspired from our ancient epics and classical literature. Have you seen some of his most famous paintings, such as *Buddha and Sujata*, *Avisarika*, *Radhika* and *Sri Chaitanya with*

His Followers on the Sea Beach of Puri? Later in his career, Abanindranath derived inspiration from Eastern countries like Japan and China and learnt to use their wash technique. This is a method in which water is used quite liberally, with the sheet of paper to be painted being dipped in water before colours are applied on it. Have you ever tried this method of painting? Try it—it's a treat to the eye and fun to do!

While Abanindranath and other Indian artists were rebelling in their own way, something big was happening in Bengal. In 1905, Lord Curzon, the viceroy of India (the head of the British government in India), announced that Bengal would be divided into two provinces—Eastern Bengal and Assam as one province, and the rest of Bengal, which included Bihar and Orissa, as the other province. As you would have guessed, this decision was met with many, many protests.

And this spirit of protest showed in the art of the time as well. It was in this environment that Abanindranath painted his most famous painting—*Bharat Mata*, or Mother India. As a concept, the figure of Mother India, evoked in the nineteenth century, is the personification of India as a mother goddess. Until now, Mother India was generally considered and painted as a protector figure looking after her children. But in Abanindranath's painting, Mother India—dressed in saffron and holding a book, sheaves of paddy, a piece of white cloth and a garland in her four hands—appeared as if she was herself in need of protection. The painting became extremely popular among the freedom-hungry Indians. It was even enlarged and transferred on to a silk banner by a Japanese artist and then carried in nationalist processions. Abanindranath's *Bharat Mata* added great vigour to the Swadeshi movement.

Like Abanindranath, his brother Gaganendranath Tagore too was a painter—and one of India's very first cartoonists. Both the Tagore brothers, with support from their uncle Rabindranath Tagore, formed the Indian Society of Oriental Arts in 1907 to promote ancient Indian art traditions.

Teacher Knows Best

There's a wonderful little story that tells us what a great teacher Abanindranath Tagore was. One day, Nandalal Bose—his student—painted something and showed it to his teacher. Abanindranath looked at it intently and said, 'Your painting is well executed, but I think you should add more colour.' The painting in question was *Uma-r Tapasya,* or The Penance of Uma.

Early next morning, Nandalal sat with his painting and paints, wondering how to add more colour. Just then, he heard the sound of a car. Abanindranath had come to see him. He began, 'Yesterday, I told you to add colour to your painting, but after you left, I realized that this was an image of a sad Uma, and therefore it shouldn't have much colour. Thinking of the painting, I could not sleep all night—I feared that you might add more colour and spoil your painting! So I rushed to see you so early in the morning.'

So of course Nandalal did not make his now famous painting very bright and colourful. However, since his teacher had suggested the use of more colour when he'd first showed it to him, Nandalal decided to add a touch of green to Uma's ring—just to follow his teacher's word. One has to look at the painting *very* closely to notice it. Have you spotted it?

Rabindranath: The Genius Called Gurudev

Apart from Abanindranath Tagore, there's one artist who was perhaps the most instrumental in the flowering of the Bengal school of art. We have all seen his images—clad in a loose robe, with a long, flowing beard and smiling eyes. We know him as Rabindranath Tagore, and as Gurudev, as he was fondly called. Rabindranath was a great poet, writer, painter and playwright. And more importantly, he was the founder of a most unusual school in Santiniketan, which became the cradle of the Bengal school of art and laid the foundation of modern art in India.

Rabindranath always believed that an artist should only be governed by what the artist wants to express and not by any formal training. In fact, he turned his lack of training in art into an advantage and created a unique childlike style of painting. To provide a space where other artists could thrive, think freely and create the kind of art they really wanted to create, in 1919, he started an arts centre called Kala Bhavana at his school in Santiniketan, which has produced some of the most renowned modern Indian artists. During his life, Tagore created over 3000 drawings and paintings, and was the first Indian artist to exhibit his works across Europe, United States and Russia.

But would you believe that Rabindranath started drawing and painting only when he was in his late sixties? Shocking, right? That's because becoming an artist was not a conscious decision for him. In fact, Rabindranath had always had an artistic bent. Even as a child, he was attracted to the various forms of beauty scattered in nature—the play of sunlight on leaves, the moving branches of a faraway tree, the changing form of a river as it flowed. And as he grew older, these keen observations found expression through art alongside what he wrote. While correcting his manuscripts, Rabindranath would doodle over the words, cover them with ink and add some lines to make irregular shapes and patterns, like free-flowing ribbons, mysterious faces and bizarre birds. And it was these little doodles and scribbles that developed over time and became one of the most iconic works that Gurudev created. Some of these fun doodles can be seen in the original manuscript of a poetry book that he wrote in 1924 titled *Purabi*. Look it up, won't you?

If you come across some of Rabindranath Tagore's famous paintings, like *Bird (Fantastic)*, *Dancing Woman* and *Vase*, you'll notice that Rabindranath's artistic works are like fairy tales—full of fantasy and rhythm. He drew some very strange-looking creatures, mystical landscapes, beasts and flowers, and many other odd subjects. And he made them freely, with brushes, rags, cotton wool and even

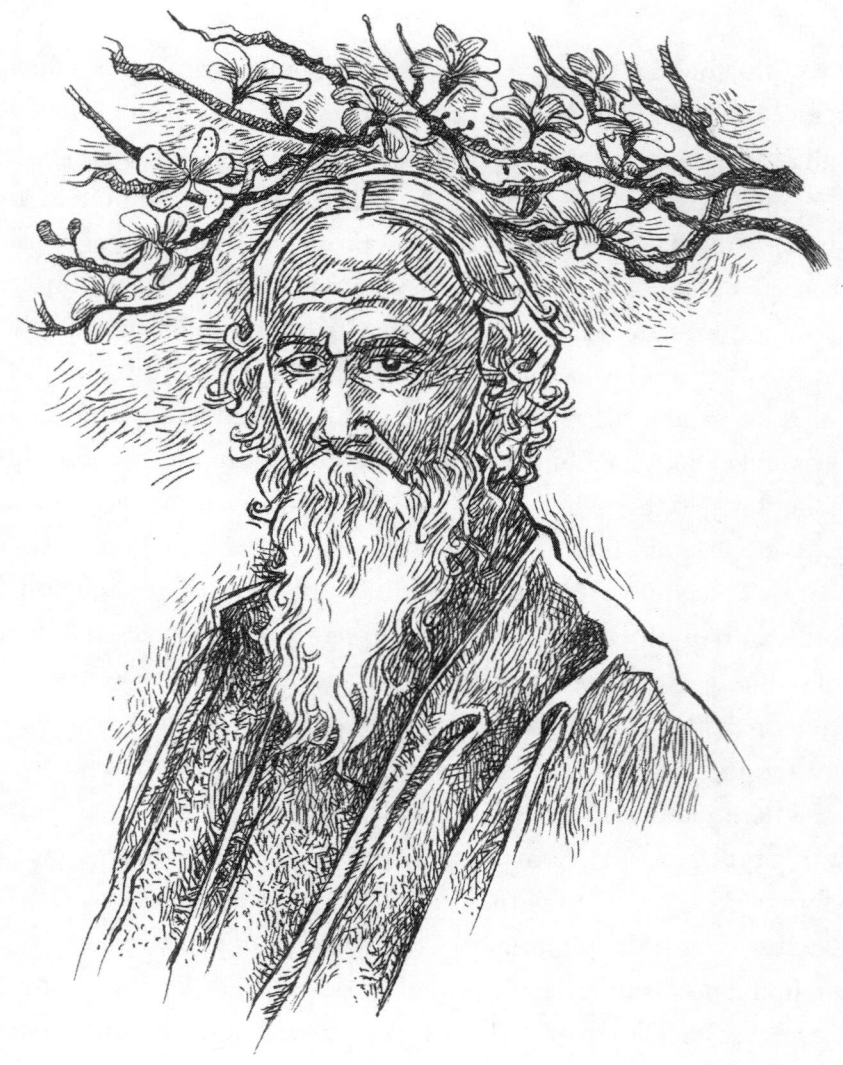

Rabindranath Tagore, when not amused by his own drawings

his fingers. The act of drawing gave Rabindranath immense joy. He sometimes even talked to his drawings and at other times laughed looking at them. Perhaps this pure joy of expressing what one feels is the reason why so many artists even create art, don't you think?

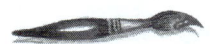

Other Gems of the Bengal School

Abanindranath was no ordinary teacher—he always encouraged his students and even appointed a scholar to recite ancient Indian epics to them so that they could draw inspiration from India's past. He created an atmosphere in which teachers and students could work together in the pursuit of art. The Indian Society of Oriental Arts even arranged exhibitions of students' works and hence provided much-needed support to young artists. At home, Abanindranath was regularly visited by his students and fellow artists, and the southern veranda of his house—where he sat and worked—became an unusual art space, called the Vichitra Art Club, where artists held lively discussions on art, poetry and music! Thus the Bengal art movement spread rapidly, and soon Abanindranath's students—famous painters Nandalal Bose, Jamini Roy, Asit Kumar Haldar and Kshitindranath Majumdar—took the tradition forward.

Nandalal: The Boatman of the Bengal School

Nandalal Bose soon became one of Abanindranath Tagore's most outstanding students. And no, he didn't row boats for a living! The word 'boatman' is just a metaphor to tell you how important a role Nandalal played in *rowing* forward the Bengal style on the mighty *river* of Indian art! From a very young age, Nandalal wanted to become a painter, and he collected all the money he could to buy books on art. He started learning drawing, particularly still life, from his cousin, who was an artist. One day, he came across a painting of Buddha in one of his books, made by Abanindranath Tagore, and he immediately knew that this was the teacher he was looking for. After taking one look at Nandalal's drawings, Abanindranath immediately accepted the boy as his pupil. And the rest, as they say, is history. Soon Nandalal became quite a name in the art world. He drew inspiration from the murals of Ajanta and Ellora, miniature paintings and the folk art forms, his artwork mostly depicting subjects from mythology, nature and village life.

When Rabindranath Tagore established Kala Bhavana, which later became part of the university of Visva-Bharati in Santiniketan, he asked Nandalal to be its principal. Nandalal was only thirty-seven at the time! As the head of Kala Bhavana, he encouraged his students to travel to different parts of the country and study the wonderful art of ancient India. It was at Santiniketan that Nandalal Bose met Mahatma Gandhi, and when Bapu led the historic Dandi March in protest against the salt tax levied by the British, Nandalal created a beautiful black-and-white painting of him. Did you know that when

The Haripura Panels

In 1938, Nandalal Bose was asked to make a series of posters by none other than Mahatma Gandhi. The Father of the Nation wanted to put these up in the pandal in Haripura, Gujarat, where the Indian National Congress was to hold a session. Today, these posters are popularly known as the Haripura panels.

A gardener, a tailor, a dhobi with a donkey, a drummer, a woman pounding rice—Nandalal Bose's Haripura panels depict ordinary people and their everyday lives.

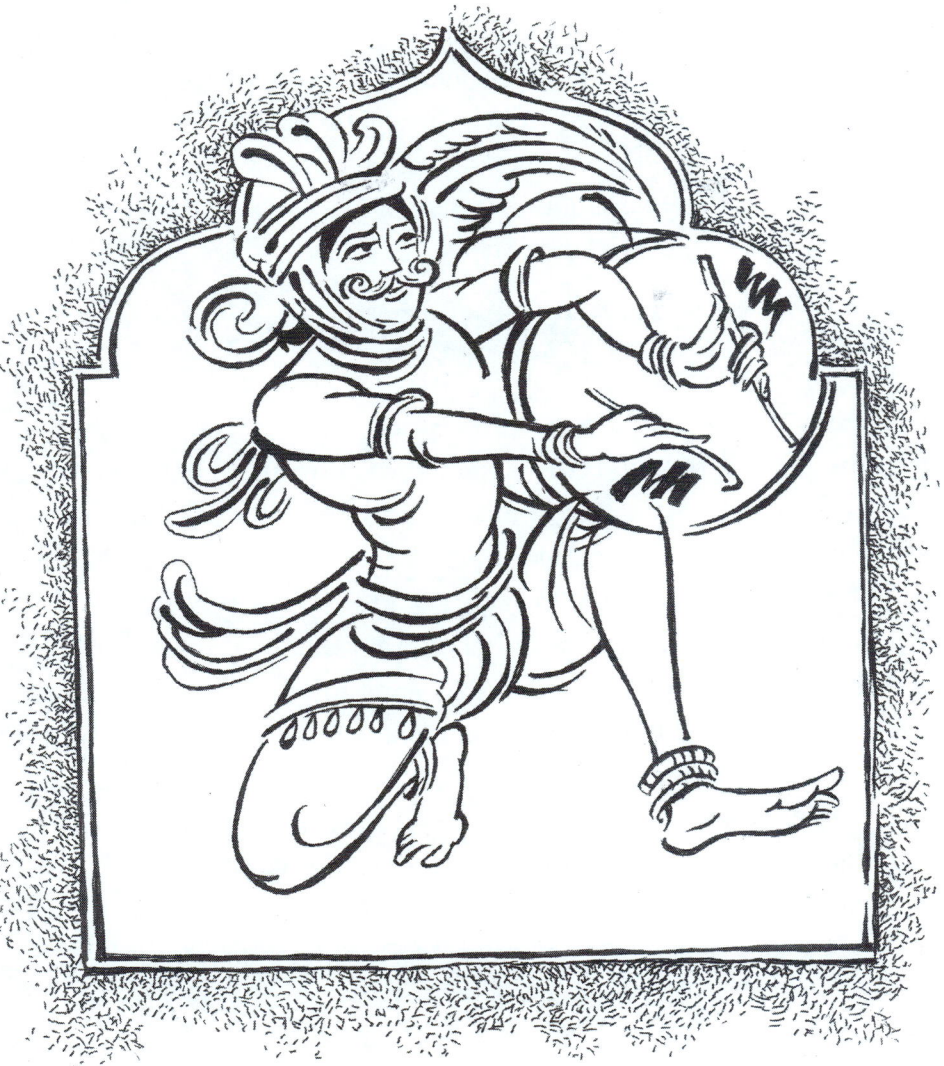

Nandalal Bose's merry drummer on a Haripura panel

the Indian Constitution was drafted after Independence, it was Nandalal Bose—along with some of his students—who decorated it with many beautiful illustrations? Nandalal Bose also drew the emblems for the Bharat Ratna and the Padma Shri, the highest awards given by the Government of India. They don't call him the boatman of the Bengal school for nothing!

Binode and Ramkinkar: The Stars of Santiniketan

At Santiniketan, Nandalal successfully revived the study and practice of Indian art. Under him, Kala Bhavana flourished and two great artists emerged from the school—the famous sculptor–painter Ramkinkar Baij, who broke away from the British style of sculpting and created sculptures inspired from the scenes of rural life he saw around him, and Binode Bihari Mukherjee, a painter who loved to try out different mediums all through his life.

Ramkinkar Baij was one of the earliest artists to bring in a bold, abstract approach to Indian sculptural forms, and he freely experimented with materials, especially cement and concrete. His works—both paintings and sculptures—are spontaneous and extremely dynamic. Many of his creations are inspired by the lifestyles of the tribal communities living in and around Santiniketan, like his famous sculpture of a Santhal family setting out to a new destination in search of work. The majestic sculpture still stands in the Kala Bhavana campus of Santiniketan.

Binode Bihari suffered from poor eyesight from his childhood and became totally blind towards the later part of his life. But even this could not stop him from painting. Imagine the courage and genius of this artist! Did you know that Binode Bihari Mukherjee also taught drawing and painting to the world-renowned film-maker and children's writer Satyajit Ray? He never let his disability stop him from learning or teaching art. Does that remind you of someone else? How about Beethoven, the great German composer? Beethoven became completely deaf in his forties but didn't let that affect his love for music, and he went on to compose some of the greatest musical masterpieces in the world. That's some outstanding dedication to the arts!

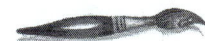

Amrita: An Artist Ahead of Her Time

While the Bengal school of art held sway in the country, there emerged a painter whose works captured a different spirit of Indian art, which was quite unlike the style of the artists of the Bengal school. Using a novel colour and form, she broke away from glorifying our rich cultural heritage— which she thought the artists of the Bengal school did—and instead painted India as she saw it.

Her name is Amrita Sher-Gil. You might know her from her famous paintings of ordinary people, mostly villagers and peasants, like *South Indian Villagers Going to Market, Hill Women, Village*

Flute Player or Banana Eater?

Binode Bihari Mukherjee once went to show one of his paintings to his teacher Abanindranath Tagore. Abanindranath looked at the painting and asked, 'What is this?'

Binode answered, 'It's a boy playing the flute . . .'

'Is he playing the flute or eating a banana?' said Abanindranath, and then asked him to show it to his brother Gaganendranath.

Gaganendranath too studied the painting and asked Binode, 'Do you even know how to play the flute?' And when Binode said he didn't, the older artist advised, 'Try playing one; only then will you understand where your painting has gone wrong.'

Talk about finding inspiration in experience!

Scene and more. But wait—if she didn't paint like the Bengal school artists, why is she in this chapter, you might ask? Well, that's because—just like the Bengal school painters—she too, in her own unique way, opposed blindly following Western ideals of painting and tried to find her 'Indian' identity through her painting style. This must have been especially significant for her because, you see, Amrita was of mixed origin—her father was Indian and her mother, Hungarian.

Amrita spent most of her childhood in Hungary and showed talent and signs of becoming a great painter from a young age. She came to India briefly and trained under her uncle in Shimla. At the age of sixteen, she went to Paris and formally learnt art at the well-known art school École des Beaux-Arts. Here Amrita was exposed to the international world of art. But she always felt a strong urge to return to her roots in India, for she firmly believed that her art should be connected to her soil. And so Amrita came home to India. And, like it was for all the great painters during her time, Mughal miniatures and the paintings of Ajanta greatly impressed and inspired her. Amrita travelled the country extensively. Her visit to south India and the various sights she encountered there have been beautifully captured in a series of paintings that she created. Domestic workers, village women and the poor were often her models, and Amrita painted them in striking colours, fusing her lessons in Western forms of art with subjects rooted in Indian culture to create some brilliant masterworks.

Sadly, Amrita died young, when she was only twenty-eight years old. She sold almost close to nothing when she was alive, but her works were later declared national 'art treasures' by the Government of India.

A Recap: Simple? Not Quite So!

The works of the artists of the Bengal school of art remain invaluable and have endured time. This was perhaps the first school representing an art movement in modern India and is, therefore, an important milestone in Indian art history. From the paintings of Ajanta to Mughal miniatures to scenes of humble village life—the artists of the Bengal school always sought inspiration from Indian history and from the reality they saw around them. All along, the artists' attempt was to be true to their own traditions—so much so that even when they perused Chinese scrolls and Japanese woodcuts for inspiration, they did not forget to merge their new insights with Indian elements. Even today when we look at these beautiful works, we can make out that each line was drawn with great sensitivity and skill, with the intention to take us back to our rich past again and again.

Catch the Real Thing!

National Gallery of Modern Art (NGMA), New Delhi, is a treasure trove of artwork created since the nineteenth century.

Where: Delhi

Entry: Rs 20 for Indian nationals; free admission for children below eighteen years of age; Rs 500 for foreign nationals

What to see: The NGMA has an entire level dedicated to the Bengal school of art, as well as over 100 paintings by Amrita Sher-Gil. Tip: Do try to see if there's a difference between Sher-Gil's earlier and later works.

Remember: Buy some postcards at the end of your visit!

Know more at: www.ngmaindia.gov.in

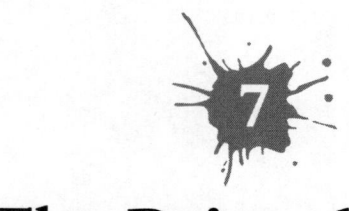

The Painted Tales

Kalighat Paintings

What do you think anger can cause? Take the wildest guess. Does it lead to getting red in the face? A heated argument? A fist fight, perhaps? Well, whatever your answer, it could not have been this: anger can also lead to the creation of a temple. Well, at least in Indian mythology, it can! How? Here's a little story . . .

On the snow-clad mountain called Kailash lived the great Hindu god Shiva with his wife goddess Sati. One day, Sati saw a large procession of gods and goddesses crossing Kailash. She was curious to know where all of them were going, so she asked one of the gods and found out that her father, Prajapati Daksha, was holding a fire sacrifice. Sati was amazed. Why had her father not invited her and her husband? Maybe he had forgotten, thought Sati. So she went to her husband and said that, invited or not, they must go to her father's house for the ceremony.

Lord Shiva accepted his wife's request. Taking Nandi the bull, his white mount, Shiva and Sati arrived at Prajapati Daksha's house. However, Sati was reluctantly received by her father, and Shiva was mocked and humiliated. You see, Sati had married Shiva against the wishes of her father. He had wanted his daughter to marry a deva, or god, rather than a yogi, or ascetic, as Shiva was considered to be. Unable to take the insults hurled at her husband, Sati got so angry that she stepped into the sacrificial fire. Looking at his wife in flames, Shiva got furious. He took Sati's burnt body in his arms and started performing the Tandava, the celestial dance of destruction.

All the gods feared that if Shiva continued to dance like this, the entire universe would be destroyed, and so they went to Lord Vishnu for help. To stop the Tandava, Lord Vishnu used his Sudarshana Chakra, a disc-like weapon, and cut Sati's body into several pieces. This shook Shiva out of his anger and he went back to Kailash to perform a severe penance for his actions.

Do you know what happened to the various parts of Goddess Sati's body after that? The story goes that the parts were scattered across India, and each spot in which a piece fell became a holy place, where people formed a Shakti *peetha*. There are fifty-one such Shakti peethas, and it is said that Goddess Sati's right toe fell in Bengal, where the famous Kalighat Kali Temple stands today. You can find the first references to this temple, situated on the ghats of River Hooghly in Calcutta, in texts written around the fifteenth century. An ancient place of worship, the Kalighat temple has an idol of the goddess Kali that has a long, protruding tongue made of pure gold!

Storytellers of Yore

You must be wondering how a temple is related to art, right? Well, let's find out! As you must know, all old structures need to be repaired and polished from time to time, and so did the Kalighat temple.

After extensive renovation in the year 1809, the temple regained importance. Since Calcutta was the capital of the British Empire, Kalighat became a magnet for locals, pilgrims and foreign visitors.

Cut to the neighbouring villages of Calcutta, where lived many artists. Based on the epics Ramayana and Mahabharata, they painted long stories, in sections, on scrolls made of cloth. Each section of the story on the cloth canvas is called a *pat*, and the complete narrative painting, a *pattachitra*. The artists who created these paintings came to be known as *patua*s. The patuas travelled from village to village and to temples, markets and festivals and, unrolling the illustrated scroll one section at a time, told, or rather sang, these stories to their audiences. As the popularity of the Kalighat temple was growing at the time, the patuas thought that it would be more lucrative for them to sell their paintings outside the temple. And so they set up small stalls outside the complex and did just that! However, the visitors—mostly the British—didn't want to buy long scrolls that took a long time to make; they wanted small paintings that they could carry as souvenirs. Therefore, the patuas started painting individual sections on machine-made paper—produced by up-and-coming paper mills—using bold, strong lines, vibrant colours and simple settings that involved just one or two figures and could be painted quickly. Drawn with a continuous sweep of paint, the figure(s) in the paintings appeared such that it was hard to see where the artist's brush may have been touched to the page and where it was withdrawn! These particular characteristics made these paintings highly remarkable and well known as—you must've guessed it by now—Kalighat paintings.

Theme Talk

Kalighat paintings were sold as religious souvenirs, hence the themes were mostly spiritual. The depiction of Hindu gods and goddesses, episodes from the Ramayana and the Mahabharata, scenes

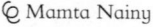

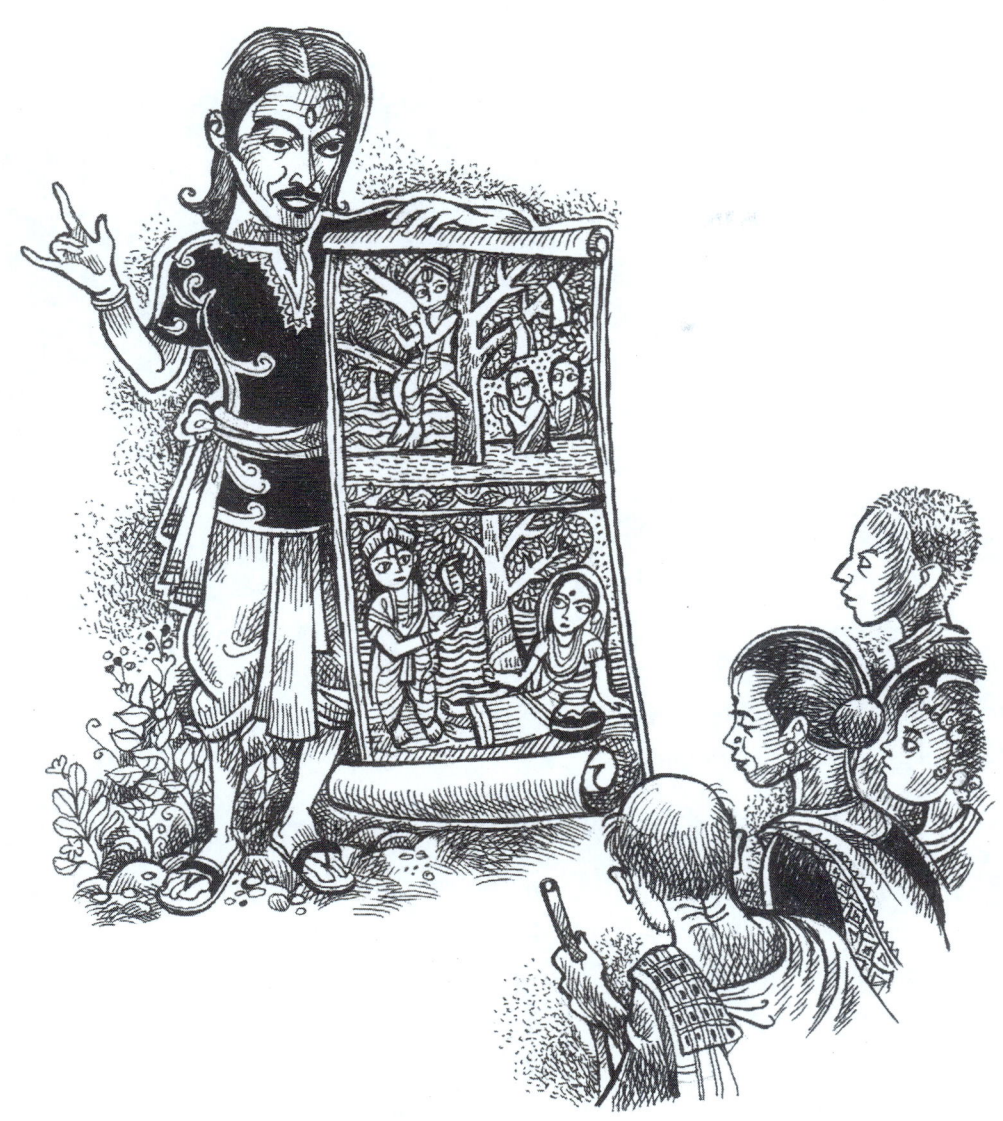

A patua regales a village audience

from the life of Lord Krishna, the various avatars of Lord Vishnu, etc. were the main subjects. But among all the deities, Goddess Kali was the patuas' favourite. They painted many an image of the goddess using indigenous colours, like yellow made from turmeric root, black soot produced by burning an oil lamp under a pot, red dye made from various flowers. Later on, when factory-made watercolours were produced by the British, the artists started using these.

Popular Creatures

Animals and birds made up another favourite theme of the patuas—which might be because of the influence of Mughal miniatures. Cats, pigeons, prawns, lobsters and fishes made frequent appearances in Kalighat paintings.

Creating a Kalighat painting was mostly a family affair, in which the women and children took care of the preparations, like grinding the colours and creating the dyes. They also made outlines in pencil and filled the basic shapes with paints. The male members of the household, who were usually the experts of this art style, did the final and complex portions of the drawings. You can say that these paintings were a result of teamwork, which is perhaps why most of the earlier Kalighat pats do not bear any signatures of the artists.

A Twist in the Tale

In the middle of the nineteenth century, Calcutta saw the rise of the upper and middle classes of society. These Western-educated, high-class, rich Indian gentlemen, called babus, were greatly influenced by the British. They tried to copy the British in their mannerisms and clothing by wearing crisp pleated dhotis and Western shoes and oiling their hair nicely.

Now, this new cosmopolitan culture of Calcutta inspired the Kalighat painters a great deal. They wanted to depict the oddities, hypocrisies and changes that the society was witnessing. And so they started experimenting with social themes. They took to drawing satirical images of the newly rich, the corrupt priests and the high-class babus. Brimming with quirky humour and symbolism, these paintings portrayed a very entertaining but real view of Calcutta's society at that time. A famous Kalighat painting, for example, is of a fat cat with a lobster in its mouth and a tilak on its forehead—symbolizing a greedy priest!

Hard Days of the Patuas

By the end of the nineteenth century, with the coming of printing techniques, it became difficult for Kalighat painters to compete with mass-produced prints. In addition to this, the Bengali upper and middle classes were increasingly becoming more appreciative of Western styles of painting, and though the patua community tried to adapt to the tastes of the babus, the popularity of Kalighat paintings slowly started declining.

But then something unexpected happened. John Lockwood Kipling, an English artist, teacher and museum curator—also the father of Rudyard Kipling (yes, the one of *The Jungle Book* fame)—came across some Kalighat paintings and was wonderstruck by them. He saw Kalighat artists not just as illustrators who drew merely what they saw around them, but as thinking artists. Through his teaching years at Sir J.J. School of Art, Bombay, and Mayo School of Industrial Arts, Lahore (in case you're wondering, Lahore—which is in Pakistan now—was a part of India then), and later, during his stint as curator of Lahore Museum, he greatly promoted Kalighat paintings. He also had a massive personal collection of these paintings and when he went back to England after spending

82

twenty-eight long years in India, he carried several of these works with him. Would you believe that today, his huge collection of Kalighat paintings lies at the Victoria and Albert Museum in London, making Kalighat art one of India's most recognized art styles the world over!

Jamini Roy: The Trailblazer

Many modern artists in the twentieth century drew inspiration from Kalighat paintings, for these works were simple yet extremely powerful. One such artist who turned to Kalighat paintings to develop his own unique style of art was the famous painter Jamini Roy, and he has a story of his own.

Born in a small village in the Bankura district of Bengal, Jamini was greatly inspired by the various forms of folk and local art traditions— like beautiful clay pottery and terracotta-toy making—that surrounded him in his village right from his childhood. Jamini was formally trained in art at Government School of Art, where he was taught by Abanindranath Tagore. Quite obviously, under Abanindranath's guidance, he began painting in the Bengal style of art, which was prevalent at that time. Jamini also made some brilliant landscape and portrait paintings in various styles. Yet he wasn't satisfied. He wanted to find his own unique style of painting. But this process was difficult and there was little to no success, and so Jamini had to endure extreme poverty. Greatly disheartened, he took up odd jobs to survive.

Rural Gone Global

Jamini Roy was an experimental artist, who even painted Jesus and Madonna and recreated the famous painting *The Last Supper* in his unique folk style!

© Mamta Nainy

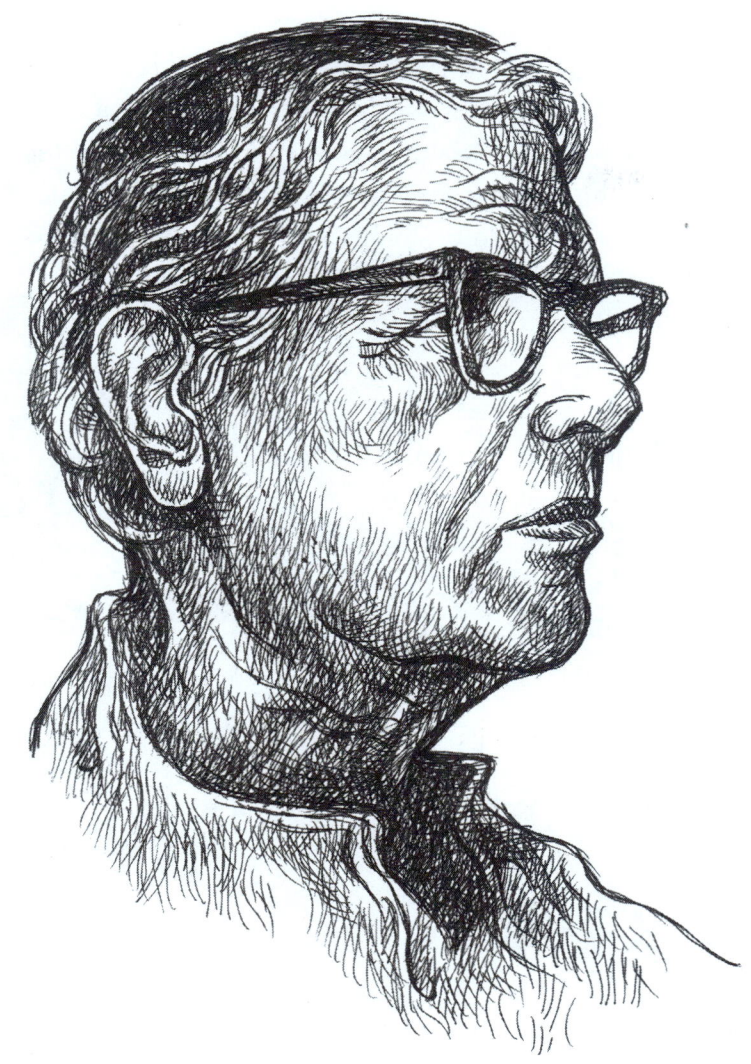

Jamini Roy turns to the Kalighat style

And then one day, he thought of travelling through the city of Calcutta in order to discover himself and his art anew . . . only to find out that the answer to his predicament lay very close to him. Yes! It was the Kalighat paintings sold outside the Kalighat Kali Temple! Jamini began experimenting along the lines of Kalighat paintings and even took lessons from patuas. He abandoned the use of foreign art materials and started using natural colours. He even made his own painting surfaces using cloth, wood and mats.

Jamini Roy's unique style of painting finally took off from Kalighat paintings and marked a new phase in the history of Indian art. He made some beautiful portrayals of folk subjects in bold, bright colours, including the Santhal tribe (an adivasi people hailing from Bengal); mythological ones, like Lord Krishna and his brother Balarama; and female figures like Radha and the gopis. He

The Perfect Palette

Jamini Roy chose a distinct colour palette of seven shades for his paintings. These colours were red, yellow ochre, green, vermillion, grey, blue and white. Imagine creating *so* many different paintings with only seven colours!

even painted the entire Ramayana in the Kalighat style using over seventeen canvasses! During his lifetime, Jamini produced—hold your breath—32,000 paintings, which is said to be bigger than any other Indian artist's body of work! And if it wasn't for the magnetism of Kalighat paintings, we wouldn't have seen the rise of such a great painter like Jamini Roy.

A Recap: Unfurling a Tradition

The Kalighat style of painting was perhaps the first kind of painting tradition in India that was modern as well as popular among all. Extremely strong yet very simple, immensely witty and possessing a certain sense of movement—all this defines the matchless style of Kalighat paintings. Even today, the practice of Kalighat paintings—the tradition of a distinct folk art, roots of which go back thousands of years or even more—continues in small villages of Bengal, where it is still being handed down through the generations.

Catch the Real Thing!

Kalighat Paintings and **Jamini Roy's Art**

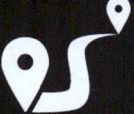

Where:
- **Kalighat Paintings:** Victoria Memorial Hall (VMH), Kolkata; Gurusaday Museum, Kolkata
- **Jamini Roy's Art:** National Gallery of Modern Art (NGMA), New Delhi; Victoria Memorial Hall, Kolkata

Entry:
- **VMH:** Rs 20 for Indian nationals; Rs 200 for foreign nationals
- **Gurusaday Museum:** Rs 2 for Indian students; Rs 10 for Indian adults; Rs 50 for foreign nationals
- **NGMA:** Rs 20 for Indian nationals; free admission for children below eighteen years of age; Rs 500 for foreign nationals

What to see: Apart from a significant collection of Kalighat paintings, the VMH also houses many masterpieces of Indian art through the ages—right from Mughal art to modern Indian paintings. Don't forget to check them out!

Remember: The VMH has a superb library with over 10,000 books. Put your reading glasses on!

Know more at: www.victoriamemorial-cal .org; www.gurusadaymuseum.org; www.ngma india.gov.in

The Makers of Magic

Other Folk and Tribal Art Forms of India

Isn't it just thrilling to come across a piece of art and recognize it immediately? It may have happened to you when you walked into a gallery and instantly recollected already having seen a work displayed there—maybe on TV, or in a book or even on your mum's sari! This chapter will feel somewhat like this. As you read on, you're sure to recognize many of the art forms mentioned in the next few pages. But where would you have already seen them, you ask? For the most part, you might know them from various textiles—bed sheets, tablecloths, cushion covers, wall hangings, outfits in your mum's wardrobe. These are the folk and tribal arts of India! Folk and tribal paintings in the country have their distinct styles—of simplified lines and dots, bright colours and basic forms, such as circles, triangles and squares—which are passed down from one generation to the next. But what *is* folk art, really?

Folk art is any traditional art belonging to a rural community in India, generally created by artisans in villages. It is the art of common, everyday people. Folk art forms are primarily functional, i.e. they are made for a special purpose, and decorative. That's why you will find that a lot of these were originally done on the walls and floors of houses. Folk art has its own unique style and no set rules (sounds like your kind of art, eh?), and this grants folk artists the freedom to go all out with their imagination, and their wit and humour too! This branch of art is also special because through it, a group or community expresses its shared values and beliefs—like stories of myths and legends, community life and birth, marriage or death rituals.

Now we come to tribal art. This is also community art but, as the name suggests, it's tribal or ancient in origin and is said to have first taken form in the depths of wilderness, away from mainstream human civilization. Home to more than 2000 tribes and ethnic groups (who practise and have their own unique culture), India is rich in tribal art traditions. Since most tribal communities hail from forests, the themes portrayed in their art depict their strong bond with nature.

Given the vastness of India, there are numerous rural and tribal communities and, as you would have guessed, as many kinds of art germinating from these diverse communities. What's more, the people, culture and geography of each group lend a unique flavour to the individual art forms. So, are you ready to test how many of these forms you already know? And for those of you who don't, let's peek into our rich heritage and savour the distinct flavours of our folk and tribal art traditions!

Madhubani: The Forest of Honey

In the north-eastern part of the Indian state of Bihar, lying between the lower ranges of the Himalayas and River Ganga, is a special place called Mithila. Legend has it that many moons ago,

Mithila was ruled by Raja Janak. Now, Janak had all the riches in the world, except for one thing that he really desired, for which he was ready to exchange all his wealth and prosperity: a baby. See, Janak and his wife were childless, and they'd tried everything—held yajnas, or ritual sacrifices, and prayed to the gods—but they'd had no luck. So, to distract himself from this unhappiness, the king decided to keep himself occupied by tending to his vast land.

One day while ploughing a field, Janak's plough got stuck in the earth. Upon looking closely, he found that the obstacle was a beautiful chest. Curious, he opened it and was stunned to find a baby girl inside! He named this baby Sita. Yes, this is *the* Sita that you've heard lots about—from the Ramayana!

Sita grew up to be a beautiful woman and when she reached adulthood, her father wanted her to find the perfect husband. So he set a test

The Chance Discovery

Sometimes even a tragic disaster can lead to something extraordinary. Take the discovery of Mithila paintings, for example. When a massive earthquake hit Bihar in 1934, the then British officer of the district of Madhubani, William G. Archer, visited the area to examine the damage caused by the quake. And that's when he chanced upon these beautiful paintings on the walls of the homes. Archer was spellbound, and he took some black-and-white photographs of these paintings. He then went on to write an article about them in the Indian art journal *Marg* and thus had a major hand in the initial popularization of the art form.

for the groom-to-be: the man who wished to marry Sita must lift an unbelievably heavy bow that once belonged to Lord Shiva. Many princes tried their luck and failed. However, there was one who succeeded. You know who, don't you? Rama, the king of Ayodhya! The wedding was planned and, as part of the grand arrangements, Raja Janak employed some local women to decorate the

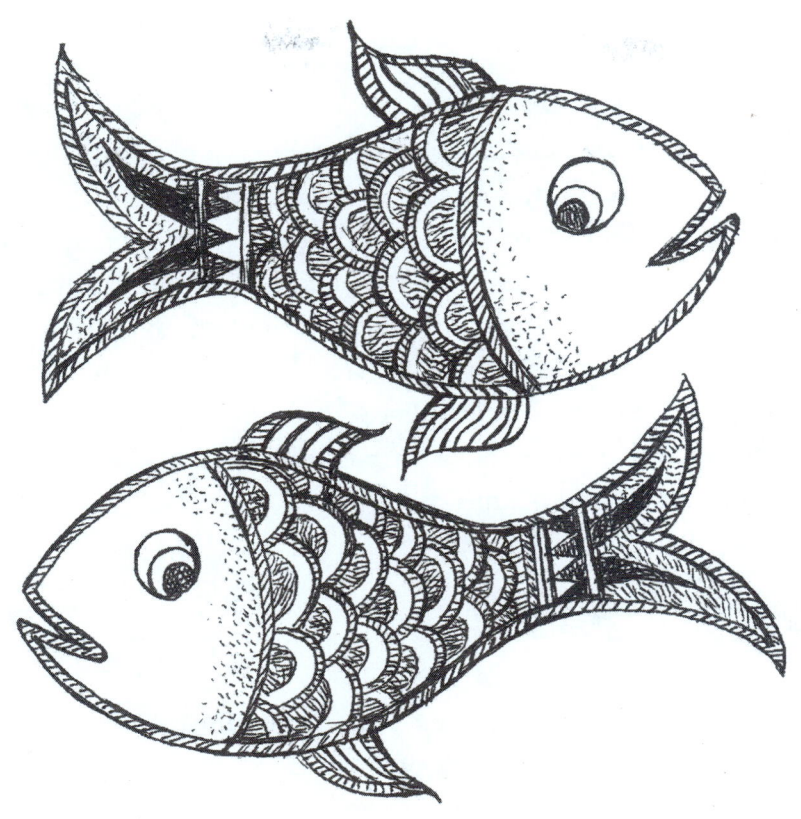

A fishy pair in Madhubani art

walls and floors of his palace. It is said that Goddess Parvati, the consort of Lord Shiva, herself helped in the decorations!

Down the centuries, the women of the Mithila region kept this tradition alive by painting on the walls and floors of their houses for festivals, ceremonies or special occasions. And this art form, having originated in the Mithila region, came to be known as Mithila paintings. You might also know these paintings as Madhubani paintings (its more popular name), which literally means 'forest of honey', since Mithila lies in the district of Madhubani.

Mithila paintings usually show double-bordered figures that have big, bulging, fishlike eyes and sharp noses. The subjects of these paintings include Hindu deities like Rama–Sita, Shiva–Parvati, Vishnu, Ganesh and Durga, or elements from nature like animals, birds, the sun, the moon, trees and flowers. Traditionally done using fingers and twigs as well as matchsticks and pen nibs, these paintings are made with bright natural colours. One look at these vibrant paintings can really cheer you up! These paintings make an appearance on many everyday objects today—from canvasses and lampshades to wall hangings and bangles.

Pattachitra: Painting on Cloth

Let's rewind to the last chapter, in which we found out how Kalighat paintings originated from pattachitras, or paintings done on scrolls of cloth, by which the traditional storytellers told mythological stories to the gathered villagers. (If none of this sounds familiar to you, this is your cue to flip the pages backwards!) Pattachitra—also the name of the art form—is one of the oldest folk art traditions of India, and is still found in Odisha, West Bengal and parts of Jharkhand and Bihar.

Patuas, the painters of Pattachitra paintings, mostly go by the surname Chitrakar, meaning 'painter'. Conventionally, these paintings were done only by men, but now they're done by women and young girls as well. However, the painter's whole family helps in the creation of a Pattachitra painting, with all the members assisting the main artist. Though originally these paintings were made on cloth, now, of course, a lot of these are made on paper too. The style of this art form is essentially handed down generations and consists of set patterns, bold lines and well-defined poses. The forms in these paintings are highly simplified and are done in vivid colours. Traditionally, Pattachitra painters used only five colours—yellow, red, green, black and white. But now they use all the different colours available in the market.

Pattachitra's themes mostly involve mythological stories, and these stories vary depending on the region and the patua's imagination. The gods and goddesses in these paintings also vary accordingly. So, for example, while a Bengali patua may prefer to paint the image of Goddess Kali or Goddess Durga (deities popularly worshipped in West Bengal), a patua from Odisha might prefer to draw Lord Jagannath (a form of Lord Vishnu that's venerated in Odisha).

It is said that Pattachitra art developed around the ancient Shree Jagannath Temple of Puri in Odisha, where the artists used to paint the temple walls with images and stories of Lord Jagannath. Over time, the base of these paintings shifted from the temple walls to cloth, so that the patuas could carry them around to relate the tales of Lord Jagannath to listeners. And then the art form travelled to the neighbouring states of Bengal, Bihar and Jharkhand.

The Fan Painting

Sometimes pattachitras are done on palm leaves. This art form is called Tala Pattachitra. The palm leaves are dried and then stitched together like the leaves of a book. The images are then inked on these leaves or panels, which can also be folded like a fan.

Did you know that Odisha's patuas make a very special pattachitra that's actually a combination of three paintings? These three paintings are of Jagannath, Balarama (Jagannath's elder brother) and Subhadra (Jagannath's younger sister), in the colours black, white and yellow respectively. The special painting of the three gods is worshipped for the duration of fifteen days every year in the month of Jyeshtha (corresponding with May–June in the Gregorian calendar), as it is believed that the deities fall ill during that fortnight, having taken a ritualistic bath on a full moon night to fight the heat of summer! How ironic that even gods fall ill!

Phad: Mobile Temples

Just like Pattachitra, Phad is a very interesting art form done on cloth scrolls, which was born some 700 years ago in the land of colours and colourful folklore—Rajasthan. There was a time when the *bhopas*—the traditional narrators or priestly singers—of the Nayak community in Rajasthan travelled across villages, carrying the painted scrolls and a lantern, to entertain the villagers. Come evening they would unravel their *phad*s, or scrolls, sing the stories aloud and even dance to them! The stories were usually about local folk heroes like Pabuji, a fourteenth-century Rajput

Curtains for Krishna

Rajasthan boasts of another famous folk art form, known as Pichwai. These devotional paintings are also made on cloth but were traditionally created as curtains for the idol of Lord Krishna, installed in a temple in the village of Nathdwara. At different times of the day, the clothes of the idol and the curtains behind it were changed. So a lot of artists settled near this temple and started creating these functional paintings.

chief who's believed to be an incarnation of Ayodhya's prince Lakshmana, and Dev Narayan, a tenth-century warrior who's believed to be an incarnation of Lord Vishnu. Traditionally, a Phad painting is thirty feet long and five feet wide, and is painted only in natural colours, using squirrel- or goat-hair brushes.

Kalamkari: Pen Drawings

There's this one folk art form that we are *so* used to seeing and wearing that we rarely ever stop to consider it as one of the finest examples of traditional art in India. You might have seen it all around you without realizing that it is a traditional art form! The name? Kalamkari, derived from the words *kalam* (pen) and *kari* (work). The Kalamkari style of painting mainly developed in two places—Srikalahasti and Machilipatnam, both in Andhra Pradesh—giving it two distinct styles. Srikalahasti Kalamkari developed near temples and has mythological themes, mainly depicting scenes from the Mahabharata, the Ramayana and the Puranas, whereas Machilipatnam Kalamkari developed under Islamic rule and therefore uses Mughal motifs like ornate floral patterns and paisley designs. Later, during the Maratha rule in Tanjore, Kalamkari art flourished further and was done on woven fabrics, out of which clothes were created for the royalty.

Traditionally, the artists created these paintings using fine pens made of bamboo. They dipped their pens in vegetable dyes before drawing the finest lines and most intricate designs on cloth. But as the art form became popular, Kalamkari artists moved away from the slow hand-drawn technique and started using carved blocks of wood to print designs on cloth. And so the Kalamkari art today includes both painting and printing.

Warli: Of Circles and Triangles

This is perhaps the simplest tribal art form, and you can try it even while reading this book . . . yeah, it's *that* simple! It's called Warli art and it is visibly similar to the stick figures of the prehistoric cave paintings. Developed by the Warli tribes of the Western Ghats, it is one of the oldest art forms of India and is usually done in white paint on an ochre background. A striking feature of this art form is that mostly simple shapes—like circles, triangles and squares—are used to depict figures. What further sets this tradition apart from the rest of India's folk and tribal art is the depiction of the human shape, which is essentially a circle and two triangles. How clever is that! You'll also notice that the faces in Warli art have absolutely no details. Warli art depicts scenes of these human figures engaged in day-to-day activities, like cooking, hunting, cleaning, harvesting, drawing water from a well, etc. This is unlike most other folk and tribal art forms, which have predominantly mythological themes.

In the past, these paintings were made by women to decorate the walls of their houses during festivals and special occasions, such as weddings or harvests. But, with time, the art form has evolved, and artists today make Warli paintings on paper, clay pots, clothes and more.

Gond: The Rhythm of Dots and Dashes

Can you imagine a stunning piece of art created just by using dots and dashes? No? Just look up Gond art on the Internet! Gond art is a tribal art form created by the Gond—indigenous peoples of central India, mainly the Vidarbha region of Maharashtra and the states of Madhya Pradesh and Chhattisgarh. The word Gond comes from the word *kond*, meaning 'green mountains', and, just as the name suggests, Gond art has been inspired by the hills, streams and forests that surround the

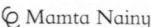

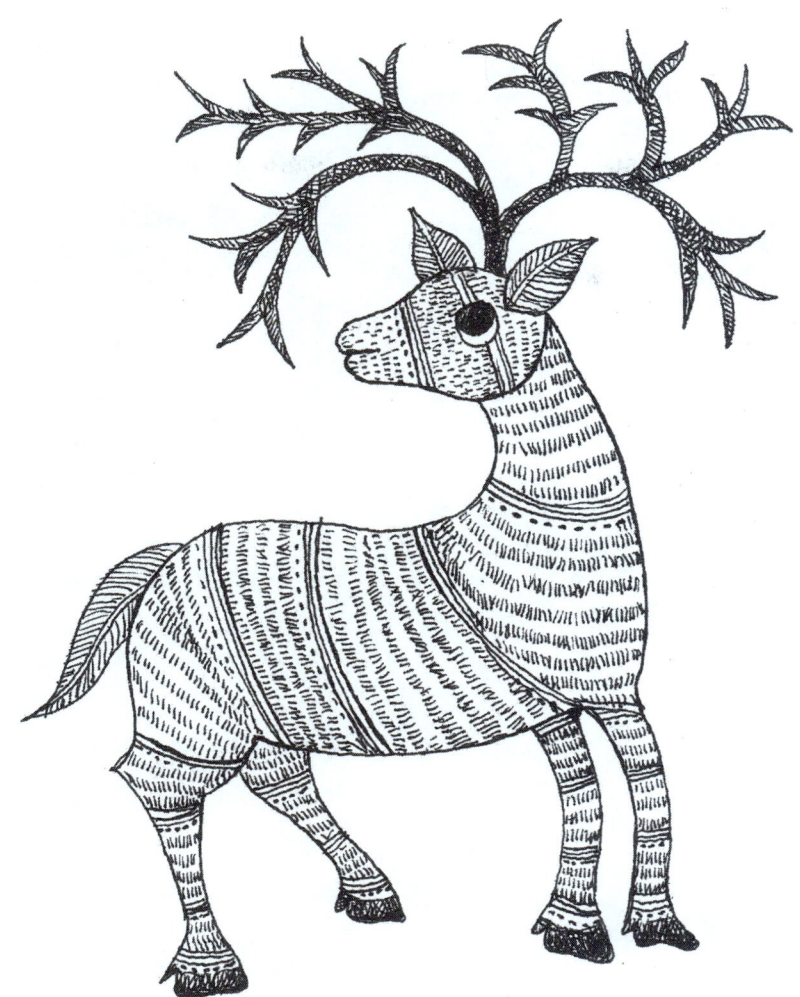

A 'dash'-ing Gond deer

Gond lands. The technique used by these artists—to depict scenes from their daily lives, or those from nature as well as myths and legends—is skilfully repeating a pattern of colourful dots and dashes to form unique motifs and designs. In fact, each Gond artist invents their own signature pattern. Would you believe that people who're familiar with Gond paintings can tell who the artist is just by looking at the signature pattern? That's some art appreciation!

These paintings were traditionally done on the walls, ceilings and floors of houses, for the Gond people believe that a good drawing brings good luck; and so they filled their homes with these wonderful images! They also made these paintings to ward off evil. But, over the years, Gond art has found its way on to paper and canvas as well.

Gold for the Gond

The Pardhan Gond were the traditional narrators in the Gond community, who painted and performed stories from Gond legends. In return, they were offered food, clothes, cattle and even gold! But when the social standing of the Gond dwindled, the Pardhan had to take up manual labour jobs to survive. That's sad, isn't it?

Here's a curious bit of information about this art form: It is believed that the technique of Gond art comes from the ancient art of tattooing, which is common in the Gond community. The Gond believe that if permanent tattoos are made on their bodies, the images will outlast their human lives—and it seems they are right, for their art is still alive and inspires awe!

Bhil: Art as Code

An art form very similar to Gond art is Bhil art. One of the largest tribal communities of India, living in the states of Madhya Pradesh, Gujarat, Rajasthan and Maharashtra, the Bhil people also skilfully

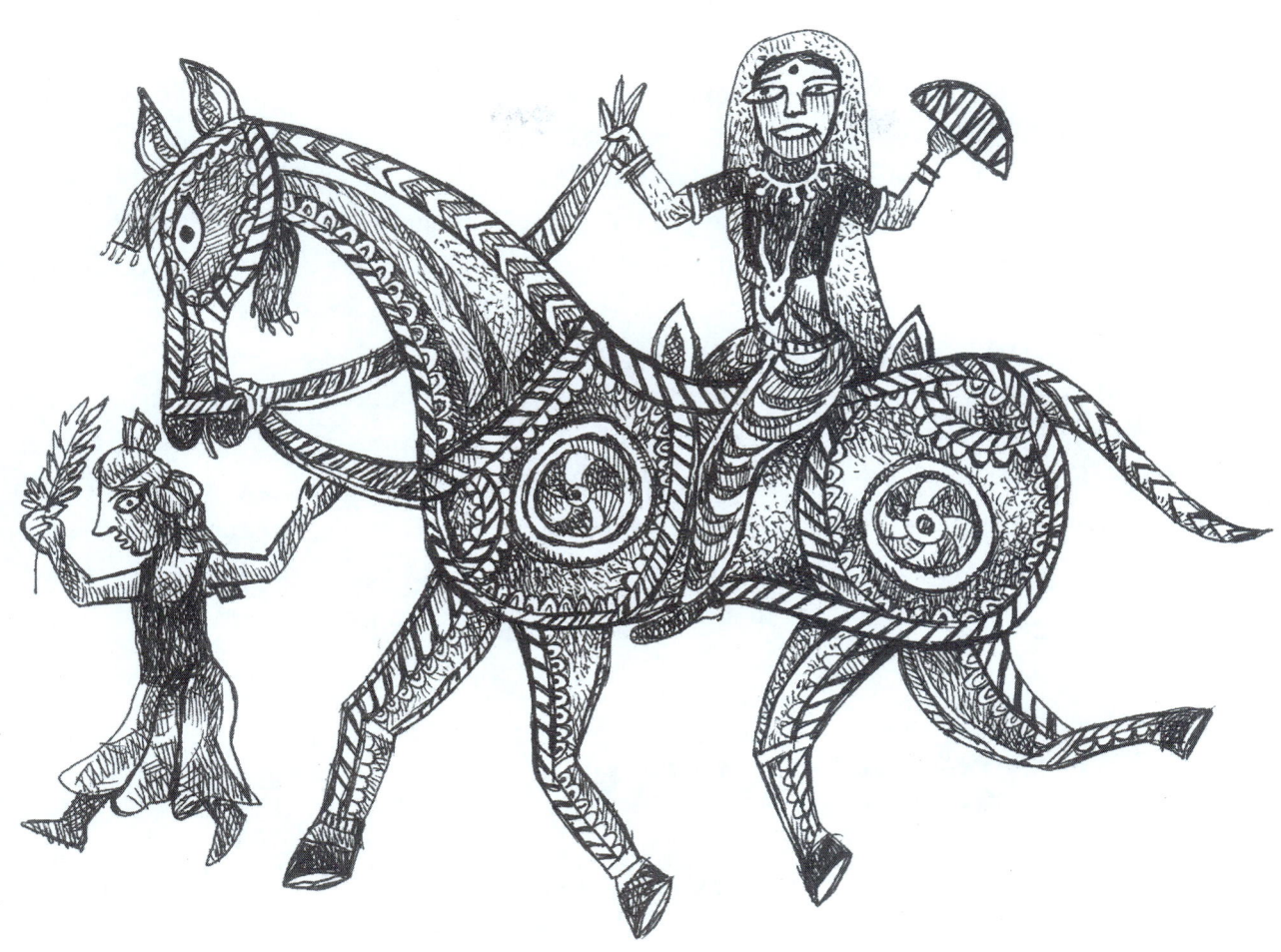

A Pithora horse to lead the way

repeat equal-sized dots in varying patterns and colours to create their unique art. It is said that Bhil art is inspired by their staple food—maize—and that each dot represents a kernel!

In the Bhil art tradition, the most widely known style is of the Pithora paintings. These are done by the sub-clan of the Bhil community—the Rathwa community, who live in the region bordering the states of Gujarat and Madhya Pradesh. Pithora is the god of the Rathwa tribe, and so the act of making Pithora paintings is highly sacred. Full of religious symbols and ritualistic motifs, the meanings behind these paintings are said to be shrouded in mystery. Some believe that each Pithora painting is a map—full of codes and symbols, such as trees, birds, the sun and the moon, animals, etc.—which serves a particular purpose.

The story goes that the roads that connected the Rathwa's habitat in the forests to nearby cities were highly dangerous. And so the Rathwa people acted as escorts and would safely lead the traders through this region in exchange for money. To make sure that the dwelling place of the Rathwa remained a secret and their livelihood protected, the leader of the community made coded maps. And these maps were made in the form of . . . Pithora paintings! If you look at the Pithora art created today, you will find that modern elements like railway tracks, aeroplanes and even computers have made their way into these paintings!

A Recap: Art from Our Own Backyard

Vibrant, detailed and brimming with simple yet intricately decorated forms, folk and tribal art in India reminds us of the most basic pleasure behind art—that of expressing oneself through it. Like so many treasures of Indian art, the folk and tribal art forms too slipped through the cracks of time along the way, but are fortunately making a comeback. They may not be as widely displayed on the walls or floors of houses, or on long scrolls of cloth in urban spaces, but they sure are visible all around us—on wall hangings, jewellery boxes, garments and other sought-after items. And while natural dyes may or may not be involved nowadays, acrylic colours definitely are. Of course, all these adaptations are mainly to do with survival purposes and are not ritualistic.

Given the sheer number of folk and tribal communities in India, most of the beautiful art forms could not be fitted in this one small chapter. In fact, there are so many communities that practise their own distinct style of art in the country that it might not even fit in several books! But then again, aren't you excited to know that there's *so* much more to learn about the vibrant folk and tribal art of India? So head to the nearest museum or get on the Internet—there's no telling when you'll be through!

Catch the Real Thing!

Most Indian states have their own museums with their local arts and crafts on display. **Indira Gandhi National Centre for the Arts (IGNCA)** hosts regular exhibitions of the folk and tribal arts of India. **National Crafts Museum (NCM)** also has many traditional arts and crafts on display.

Where: Delhi

Entry:
- **IGNCA:** Free entry for all
- **NCM:** Rs 10 for Indian nationals; Re 1 for students; Rs 150 for foreign nationals; free for students in a group and the physically challenged

What to see: The NCM is a brick-paved village complex that houses a wonderful collection of folk and tribal arts and crafts from across India. If you're lucky, you can also catch some artists demonstrating their art right then and there. And don't forget to go to the amazing cafe adjoining it as well as the museum store!

Did you know: There's a museum of Mithila paintings in Japan, which has approximately 850 Mithila paintings on display!

Know more at: www.ignca.nic.in; www.nationalcraftsmuseum.nic.in

Art Switches Gears

Meet the Moderns

Have you ever heard someone (or yourself) say, 'Oh, I could paint that!' or 'Looks like my kid sister did it!' or 'I don't really get it!' while looking at a piece of art in a museum or an art gallery? Well, if you did, chances are you were looking at a piece of modern art. But don't just go by looks, as these modern paintings are very well thought out, full of meaning, highly tough to create and reflective of the time they were made in. These modern paintings too have amazing stories to tell.

If you go by the definition of the word 'modern', then it should refer to the present, right? But a lot of these 'modern' Indian paintings were made some fifty–sixty years ago! So what is it exactly that makes modern art 'modern'?

Well, the trick to making sense of modern art is to understand that when artists and art historians discuss modernism in the field of art, they are not talking about the present day or the here and now (hint: they use the word 'contemporary' to refer to the present), but to a period when art took a crucial turn in history. And generally, any essential turn in history—which could be the result of either a single genius exploring a new artistic approach or of a group of like-minded artists following a school of art—leads to a unique idea, which, in turn, creates an entire movement.

In Indian art history, the crucial turn that led to the birth of modern art came about in the mid-twentieth century, when the country was on the brink of Independence. This was the time of patriotism and revolts and the freedom movement. This marked a truly new period in Indian art history, when the direction of art was no longer dictated by religion or tradition, as it was for the previous schools of art, but by the artists themselves.

Bengal's Story of Terrible Hunger

Though it would be fair to say that the first attempts to look at art differently and move away from traditionally Western artistic approaches began with artists like Rabindranath Tagore, Jamini Roy and Amrita Sher-Gil, the real quest to find a new way of expressing the change in Indian society through art began in the year 1943 in Calcutta. It was the year Bengal was ravaged by a terrible famine that killed millions of people.

Blamed on faulty policies of the British Empire, this devastation made several artists in Calcutta

The Young Turks

Besides the Calcutta Group, another group of artists came together in Bombay around the same time. Called the Young Turks, they were encouraged by the then principal of Sir J.J. School of Art, Charles Gerrard, to hold their first art show in 1941.

The artists in the group were against the realistic approach of the past and believed experimentation—trying out new ideas or methods—to be the most important aspect of art.

look for a new approach to art—away from the nostalgic, traditional and sentimental approach of the Bengal school—that could portray what they were seeing around them. They wanted to create art that reflected the current harsh times and also the looming changes in the country. And so, artists began to paint images that evoked the pain that was caused by the famine. During this time, some artists from the city formed a group called the Calcutta Group, and they started sharing their ideas and emotions about the social and political situation of the country through their art. The leading members of this group were Pradosh Das Gupta, Subho Tagore, Paritosh Sen, Gopal Ghose, Nirode Mazumdar and Zainul Abedin.

Outside this group, there was an artist who witnessed and recorded the Bengal famine like no other. His name was Chittaprosad Bhattacharya. He was a full-time artist for the publication division of the Communist Party of India and was sent to Midnapore, a district in present-day West Bengal, to report on the famine. There, he kept a picture journal, later published as *Hungry Bengal*, of the many victims of the famine he encountered during his stay. Chittaprosad's illustrated journal, which looks like a graphic novel, showed in simple black strokes the reality of famished children, barren trees and dead animals, telling the ugly story of extreme food shortage and terrible hunger during the Bengal famine of 1943.

New Art at the Midnight Hour

On 15 August 1947, at the stroke of midnight, the Indian tricolour replaced the British Empire's Union Jack and, after nearly two centuries of painful struggle for freedom, India finally gained independence. A free nation emerged, brimming with hope and optimism. But this independence came at a heavy cost—the Partition of India. On 14 August, a new country called Pakistan had

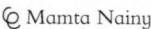
Mamta Nainy

been created on religious lines, by dividing India into two dominions; and so tens of thousands of people were displaced across the new borders.

The country was indeed undergoing a change, and this brought about a change in the world of art too. The artists of this time wanted to establish a new way of expressing themselves; they wanted absolute freedom in *what* they painted and *how* they painted. They wanted to zoom in on the realities of the new nation—urban life, poverty and the after-effects of Partition—and show the grim truths (as well as the beautiful ones) that hadn't been covered by the artists before them. 'Freedom' to them also meant freedom of expression—and these artists wanted to be independent from the traditional art forms and approaches, to create art in new and experimental ways. All this led to the formation of various artists' collectives or groups, who worked together to establish a new style of art that was both international and modern.

Bombay Art, Forward March!

One such artists' group that was formed soon after Independence, in 1947 by a few artists in Bombay, was called the Progressive Artists' Group (PAG). The group believed that Indian art should move ahead and experiment with new styles rather than revel in the past, in the way they thought the painters of the Bengal school of art did. They also wanted their art to be international—something that breaks down geographical and cultural barriers, and appeals to people across the world—and express their ideas and feelings only through stark lines and colours. PAG was averse to painting real or recognizable objects. The six founding members of this group were F.N. Souza, K.H. Ara, S.K. Bakre, S.H. Raza, H.A. Gade and M.F. Husain, and each of them emerged as a distinguished modern artist.

It was Francis Newton Souza who first came up with the idea of the Progressive Artists' Group. Born in Goa, Francis grew up in Bombay and was keenly interested in art right from his childhood. He joined the prestigious Sir J.J. School of Art but was expelled from the college for participating in the Quit India Movement in 1942. It was then that he went on to form the Progressive Artists' Group and invited his friends to join as well. The group's first exhibition was held in 1948. A rebellious artist, Francis usually chose subjects that were considered taboo in Indian society back then, like beggars, gamblers, nude figures. But the artist's most powerful paintings depict Jesus Christ, such as his famous painting *Last Supper*, which is his take on Leonardo da Vinci's celebrated painting of the same name. (Do you recall from the previous chapter that Jamini Roy also painted his version of *The Last Supper*? Go online and look at all three paintings—see how their styles differ!) When Francis was in his fifties, he moved to England and later to New York, and became a hugely popular artist worldwide.

The second member of the group was Krishnaji Howlaji Ara. He was the son of a bus driver and lost his mother quite young, and he took to earning a living by cleaning cars. But he also painted in his spare time. The budding artist was encouraged by an art critic friend to pursue painting seriously, and he took up the advice. As a member of the Progressive Artists' Group, Krishnaji held many exhibitions with the other members. But would you believe that, despite his success, this great yet humble artist continued to live and paint in a small room throughout his life? From the privacy of his room, he churned out masterpieces one after the other, of which he's best known for his female forms and still life (this basically means painting everyday inanimate objects, like flower vases, food, books, etc.). Some of his paintings, like *Window Light* and *Breakfast Table*, show a wonderful arrangement of familiar things—flowers, fruit, furniture—in a very unusual way and are a delight to the eyes!

Sadanand Bakre studied at Sir J.J. School of Art and was both a painter and a sculptor. He had a special flair for portraiture and experimented greatly with the art of sculpting. And it was Krishnaji who convinced him to become the third member of the Progressive Artists' Group. Sadanand wanted to invent new ways of creating art. And so, instead of showing people and things as they looked, he started twisting their forms using jagged shapes, thick and bright paints and bold outlines in such a way that they communicated strong feelings and emotions. Some of his outlandish but superb paintings include *Midday Sun in London*, *Landscape with Blue Sky* and *Landscape with Houses*.

The fourth member of the group was Sayed Haider Raza. He studied painting at Nagpur School of Art and Sir J.J. School of Art. An extremely sensitive painter, he's best known for his *bindu* (dot) paintings. These are works that use a bindu to depict a whole lot of things. How Sayed arrived at a bindu for his paintings' subject is a very interesting story: When Sayed Haider Raza was just a little boy, he could never concentrate on his studies. While in school, his mind wandered off to the trees and birds outside the classroom window. In order to fix his lack of concentration, Sayed's teacher drew a dot on the wall and asked him to focus on it. This dot later became an inspiration for many of his paintings! In case you're wondering what all a mere dot can stand for, take a look at some of Sayed Haider Raza's paintings, like *Bindu Panch Tatva*, *Shanti Bindu* and *Raktashyam*— you'll be greatly surprised!

Hari Ambadas Gade was brought into the Progressive Artists' Group by Raza. He studied science in Nagpur and then went on to teach for five years, before enrolling himself at Sir J.J. School of Art to study painting. He was a pioneer of abstraction, which means his work strove to simplify forms and did not represent any recognizable objects, but instead focused on his energy, emotions and the way he saw and felt colours and shapes. Do you know that even a stick figure made of lines and a circle is an abstraction? Just by the use of simple lines, doesn't it manage to tell you that it's a human figure without actually having to detail out an entire human body? So, Hari Ambadas Gade's paintings expressed what he *thought* and *felt* rather than what he *saw*. The colours in his paintings are what he's best known for. He initially painted in watercolours and then moved to oil paints. He loaded the colours thickly on his canvasses—and if you run your fingers over some of his works, you'll be able to feel the dips and ridges caused by the application of the thick paint! Haribabu loved travelling, and some of his travels resulted in famous paintings, like *Omkareshwar*, *Coastal Town*, *Rathasaptami*, *Gulmohar*, etc.

The sixth member of the group was—somebody we've all heard of—Maqbool Fida Husain. Born in a town called Pandharpur in the Solapur district of Maharashtra, Husain moved to the big city, Bombay, at the age of twenty, when he got admission at Sir J.J. School of Arts. During his early days in Bombay, he had to struggle a great deal to earn even a single square meal a day, and he often slept on footpaths! Did you know that this great artist once painted film posters and also worked in a children's toy factory to make a living? However, slowly but surely, Husain's

Husain's Horse Syndrome

Maqbool Fida Husain must have created hundreds of paintings of horses over the course of his long artistic career. *Sprinkling Horses*—his iconic painting of galloping horses, with their manes flying and tails in the air, drawn in a few bold strokes—is perhaps what most people associate modern Indian art with.

works started gaining wide acclaim. His bold lines, bright colours and heavy brushwork came to be recognized as his signature painting style. Elements like horses, female figures, eternal cities (like Benares) and classical myths (like the seven horses drawing the chariot of the Sun God) dominated his work. This world-renowned artist had one zany habit—he always walked barefoot and carried a huge paintbrush that he sometimes used as his walking stick! Did you know that M.F. Husain was also a film writer and director? He found his muse in the famous Bollywood actress Madhuri Dixit and watched her movie *Hum Aapke Hain Koun..!* sixty-seven times! He liked Madhuri so much in the film that he even created a series of paintings of her!

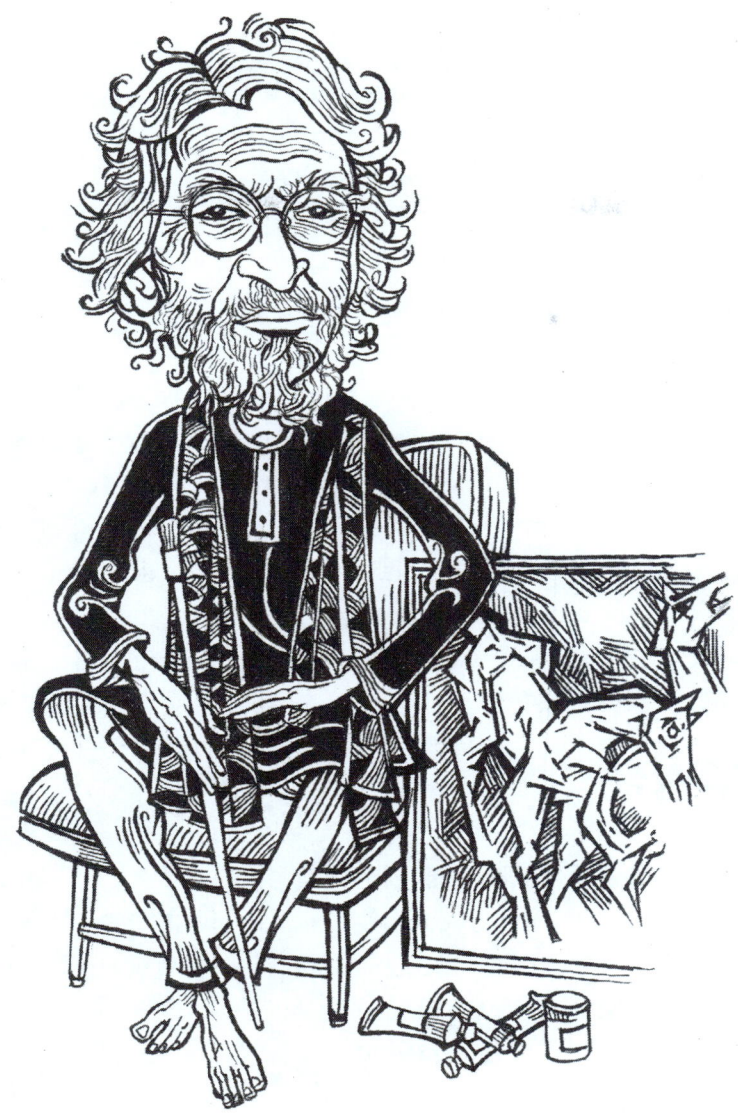

When M.F. Husain picked horses over Madhuri

Besides these founder members of the Progressive Artists' Group, there were other important modern artists during this time too, like Akbar Padamsee, Tyeb Mehta and Krishen Khanna, who supported the PAG and took forward the group's ideas of art.

Delhi's Modern Stride

The formation of the Progressive Artists' Group in Bombay was followed by a similar attempt in the city of Delhi by the painter–sculptor Krishna Shamrao Kulkarni. Born in Belgaum, Karnataka, and educated at Sir J.J. School of Art, Kulkarni, along with some other artists, started an art collective or group called the Shilpi Chakra to give the city's young artists a platform to experiment. To promote modern art, the members of Shilpi Chakra organized exhibitions of their works in small neighbourhoods and sold their paintings to the common people. And those who could not afford a straight purchase could even hire the artworks or buy them on instalments!

The Baroda Wave

Soon after Independence, Bombay became the epicentre of Indian art . . . till a significant thing happened in Baroda, Gujarat, in 1950: the opening of the faculty of fine arts in Maharaja Sayajirao University of Baroda. The college soon became a vibrant and creative hub for gifted artists from all

Female Power

This time period also saw the rise of many women artists, like Arpita Singh, Zarina Hashmi and Nasreen Mohamedi. Not only did they come forward on the artistic stage, but they also addressed women's issues in their works.

over India. Many prominent artists of the time, like Narayan Shridhar Bendre and Jeram Patel from Bombay and Kalpathi Ganpathi Subramanyan from Santiniketan, came on board as teachers. They inspired students to experiment with their art by telling stories through their images. Isn't that good advice? You should try it too—tell a story using *only* your drawings! They also encouraged the students to observe and sketch scenes from daily life as seen in the streets, markets and railway stations. And in the late fifties, as a result of the coming together of some great artists, the Baroda Group of Artists was formed. Some of the most well-known artists of this group were Bhupen Khakhar, Gulam M. Sheikh and J. Swaminathan.

Modern Art Reaches Madras

Meanwhile in south India, art took a turn for the modern when reputed painter and sculptor Debi Prasad Roy Chowdhury came down from Bengal as head of the then Madras School of Arts. He carried with him—as a disciple of Abanindranath Tagore—the traditions of the Bengal school of art. The artist stayed in Madras (present-day Chennai) for thirty years and, during this time, he tried to take forward the ideas of the Bengal school, which he combined with a great deal of experimentation. Debi Prasad was quite a maverick artist. Once, he dropped some coffee on his canvas and, instead of discarding the canvas, he asked for more cups of coffee, which he then emptied all over the canvas and created a unique painting! He also encouraged his sculpting students to experiment with various mediums, like bronze, concrete, gravel and cement. One of Debi Prasad's most iconic sculptures is *Gyarah Murti*, depicting Mahatma Gandhi with ten followers on the Dandi March, installed in Delhi.

While Debi Prasad was instrumental in bringing modernism to Madras, it was Kovalezhi Cheerampathoor Sankaran Paniker (better known as K.C.S. Paniker) who pioneered a new trend in painting in south India after succeeding Prasad as the principal of Madras School of Arts.

He formed the Cholamandal Artists' Village, which is a one-of-a-kind residential complex situated on the way to Mahabalipuram, Tamil Nadu, originally housing a community of artists who wanted to create modern art with an Indian sensibility. At Cholamandal, artists approached modernism by returning to their traditional roots in their works, looking at folk art for inspiration, using folk techniques and considering traditional styles anew.

Calcutta's Art Is Born Again

You must be wondering what was happening in Calcutta, the centre of art before Independence, right? Once the capital of British-ruled India, though Calcutta had emerged as the cradle of Indian modernism—with artists like Rabindranath Tagore and Jamini Roy—in the fifties and sixties, the artists in Calcutta felt the need to keep up with the changing times and also wanted a more independent space to practise art. So now they tried to fuse older traditions of Indian art with modern interpretations. They built on the aesthetics of the Bengal school by looking for inspiration from their own culture while steering clear of restrictions that would hamper their artistic pursuits. Theirs was an individual approach to art; their images were drawn from various sources and each artist was free to explore, experiment and develop their own styles. Some of the artists of this time period were Nikhil Biswas, Ganesh Haloi, Somnath Hore, Bikash Bhattacharjee, Ganesh Pyne and Jogen Chowdhury.

A Recap: The New World

The many collectives as well as individual artists made major contributions to the modern art movement in India by seeking a new form or style that could best describe the reality of a newly democratic nation. Indian artists had discovered and were continuously discovering their individual styles, and many novel ideas and talents came forward. So with modern art's emergence in India after Independence, the art scene in India changed completely. Cities like Delhi and Bombay, which did not have a single art gallery till 1947, suddenly became home to several galleries and museums, where the works of upcoming artists were displayed. Even the smaller cities and towns started opening galleries. And then there was the spurt of artists' groups. Though many of these collectives and groups disbanded not long after their formation, they achieved what they had set out to do: give a new direction to Indian art—a direction that led to the future.

Catch the Real Thing!

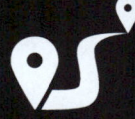

National Gallery of Modern Art (NGMA), New Delhi

Where: Delhi

Entry: Rs 20 for Indian nationals; free admission for children below eighteen years of age; Rs 500 for foreign nationals

What to see: The NGMA has an entire level dedicated to the modern artists! Examine their works and develop your own interpretation of them. See if there's a difference in the earlier and later works of these modern artists in terms of theme, style and colour palette.

Remember: Don't try to see everything. Looking at art demands attention, and it is a better idea to look at a few paintings carefully than to breeze past everything. You can always come back another day to take a look at the rest of the pieces!

Know more at: www.ngmaindia.gov.in

Art in the New World

Meet the Contemporaries

The Line between Present and Past

Have you ever wondered how long it takes for the present to become the past? A year, a decade, a century . . . or perhaps just a minute, or even a millisecond? Isn't what you did only a minute ago also history? If we go by this logic, all that was once new must inevitably turn old, and all that was once modern must encounter something even *more* modern in the future. This holds true for art too. In fact, the quest for something 'new' and 'different' in the world of art is as old as art itself!

In the late eighties, art took another new turn and fanned out in all directions, on the lookout for more diverse forms of artistic approaches. The discussions regarding subjects, themes and styles that dominated the art scene of earlier decades slowly faded away, and the younger generation of artists engaged themselves with new concerns. Is a piece of art something that you only 'look at'? Or can it be something—like a process—that you 'participate in'? Can art be created with things other than paints and brushes? Who decided what a work of art is? These were some of the questions that these artists started seeking answers to.

And as the nineties roared in, the Indian economy opened up to the world, with fast-food joints like McDonald's and Pizza Hut (you know *these* guys, don't you?) setting up shop in India. The country became globalized, and radical developments in technology and transportation came about. The way people lived, worked and travelled changed; this gave them access to new thoughts and ideas from around the globe and expanded their worldview. As a result, the world became more diverse and dynamic. Change even took place in the sphere of art; and to capture this melting pot of a world on canvas, once again artists tried to discover and develop their individual styles that would be reflective of their vision of the shifting world. And so the ideas and concepts behind a work of art became more important than the traditional values of beauty and craftsmanship in art.

The Birth of Contemporary Art

What is contemporary art? Simply put, contemporary art basically refers to art that is produced *today*. But wait up! Though it might sound quite simple, the definition of contemporary art can sometimes get a little puzzling as the interpretation of 'today' may differ from person to person. Therefore, the exact starting point of contemporary art is still largely debatable. However, many art scholars and historians believe that contemporary art refers to art created after the 1980s till the present day.

By the above definition then, contemporary artists are those who are living and creating art *now*, in the present time. And these artists are making pieces that showcase their own opinions and ideas, in their individual, exclusive styles. They are different from the artists of the previous eras,

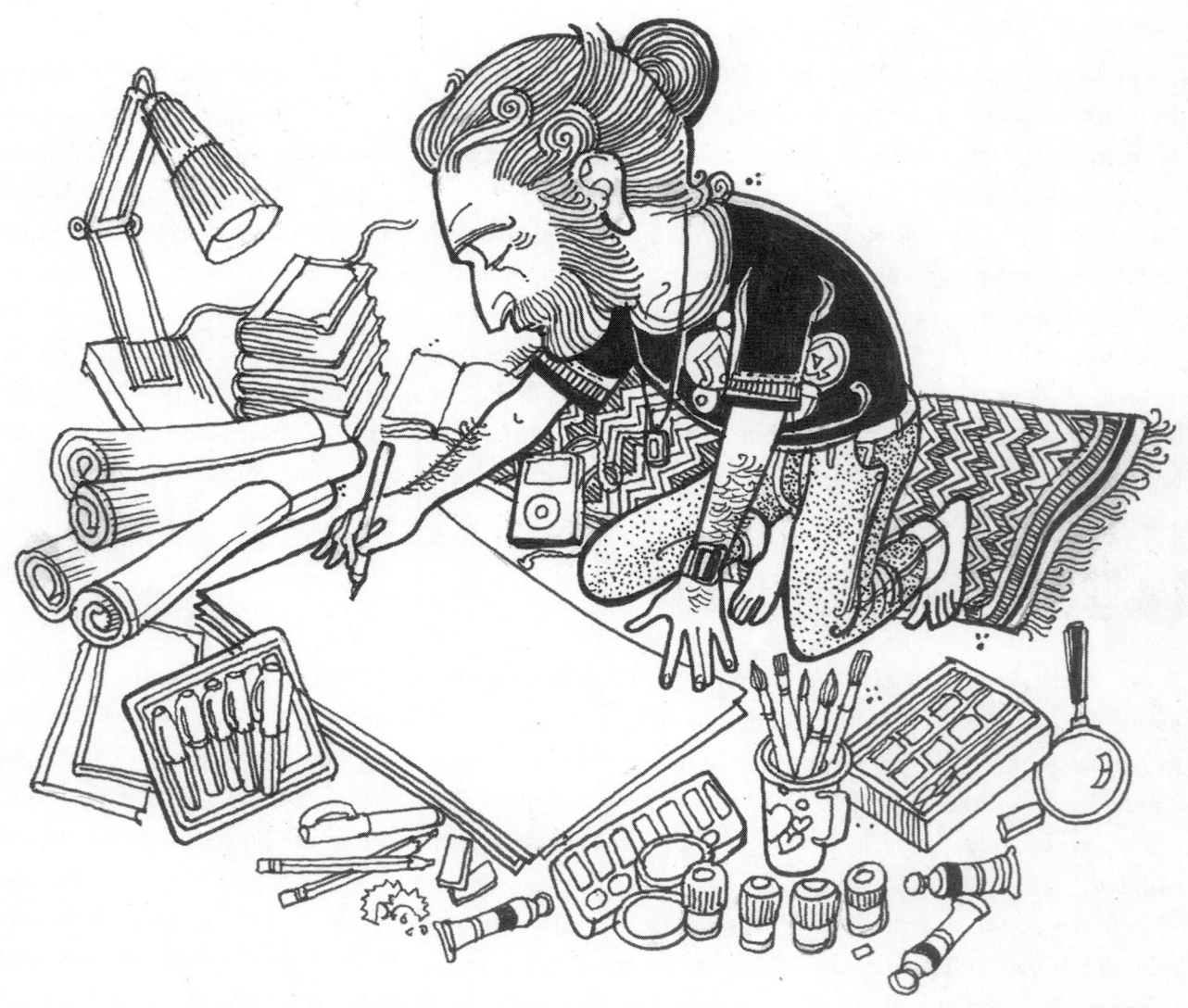

A contemporary artist tries to crack his signature style

periods and movements (who created paintings and sculptures that reflected the style of a school of art and did not particularly concentrate on individual style), as they do not believe the role of art is to encourage people to look at the world in a certain way. From art centred around religious and mythological themes to that portraying patriotic sentiments and social reforms to modern art that challenged the notion that art must realistically depict the world, the baton of Indian art has now been passed on to contemporary artists, who are turning the very idea of art on its head!

Contemporary artists try to get people to think about current events or ideas in new ways, as well as bring in the present social, personal or cultural context in their works. They try to show life in unexpected forms and ask questions that haven't been posed before. However, contemporary art doesn't always have to be art with a message. Contemporary artists also strive to recreate an experience through their art, which the onlooker can be part of, via many different approaches. They attempt to challenge the ideas of *what* art is, *how* to create art and *why* an artist creates art.

Brand-New Mediums for Brand-New Artists

Have you seen paintings made using eggshell or elephant poop, and scratched your chin? Or come across sculptures made of stainless steel thalis and *dabba*s, and found yourself at sea? Well, don't be confounded any more because now you know that,

From Bindu to Bindi

Just how Sayed Haider Raza struck upon a bindu when he was looking for inspiration, contemporary artist Bharti Kher too found her muse in the dot. She was greatly intrigued by the idea of the bindi that many Indian women wear on their foreheads, and explores its various interpretations in her art.

since art can be anything, *everything* is a valid medium! Bored with old mediums, such as oil on canvas, a lot of artists today dabble in what's called new media. Anything under the sun—old motor parts, empty bottles or even food ingredients—can be counted as new mediums of today's art. So the term 'new media' is as broad as your imagination and can include whatever you can think of—and even all that you can't!

Yes, it might seem a little strange and sometimes even funny to find people in museums admiring something as mundane and everyday as a cola can or a messy, unmade bed, but that's contemporary art—it's more about the *idea behind the art* than about the actual object. Even behind the most regular object may be an awe-inspiring concept. It could be something to do with the shapes, colours or the story it tells. Even the most ordinary image can bring out a deep emotion and, in turn, become a cause of inspiration. So the next time you come across a piece of contemporary art that you cannot understand, try thinking about the idea behind it and recognizing what emotions it brings out in you.

As you've progressed through this book, in whatever order—though this chapter shouldn't be your first!—you must've realized that the term 'Indian art' has been defined and redefined several times over. The same is true for Indian art history as well. Today, as Indian art is no longer based purely on ideology or tradition, contemporary Indian artists are drawing inspiration from the world around them as well as their roots. These contemporary artists explore their own realities—such as the plight of the common man, themes involving gender or urban crisis—through many different modes: from painting to installation to video to printmaking to photography to performance and everything in between. There are several notable Indian artists, each with their original and contemporary style, who have gained global renown, such as Anish Kapoor, Bharti Kher, Subodh Gupta, Nalini Malani, Dayanita Singh, Shilpa Gupta, Vivan Sundaram, Jitish Kallat, Anjolie Ela Menon, Jatin Das, Arpana Caur, Manjit Bawa, Manu Parekh and Atul Dodiya.

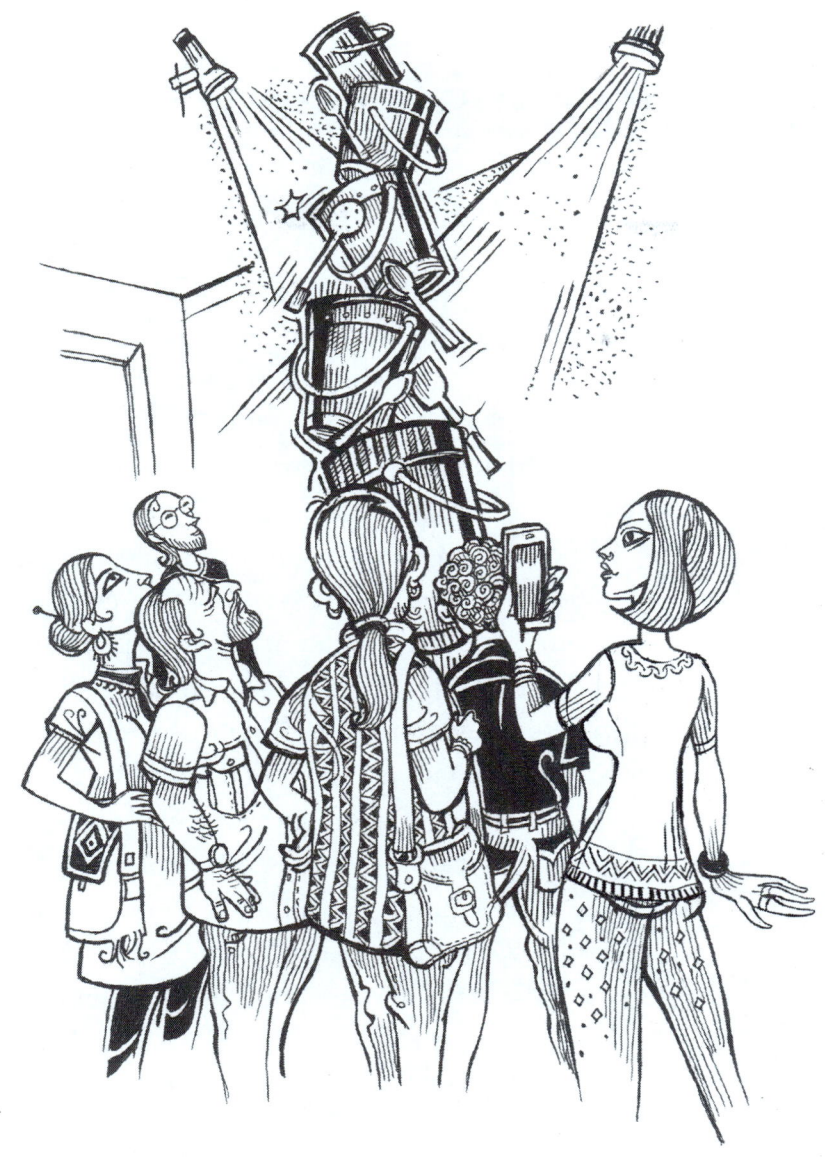

Onlookers flock around an installation artwork and attempt to decipher it

The Many Faces of Contemporary Art

Imagine if all the characters of a painting jumped out of the frame and walked about the museum. Would it still be art or would it now be theatre? Or a combination of both, perhaps? Performance artists raise these questions and use their bodies in all sorts of ways to create art. Sometimes they even dress up, have different props as well as changing settings to create scenes. They try to break down the barriers between art and life by bringing everyday activities into their work. In doing this, do you know what else becomes part of their work of art? The audience!

There's also something called installation art in the contemporary art scenario, in which art is mounted or placed in a public spot, such as a park or a museum. These are often large sculptures in myriad forms and utilize a variety of materials. Installation art is usually not meant to be permanent; it is displayed for a limited period of time and then taken away. Now, if you took down a painting from your house and moved it to another house, the painting itself wouldn't change, right? That's because a painting exists separately from its surroundings. However, there is site-specific art too, which is designed for a particular place and uses unique or specific things from the space as part of the art piece. See—*this* is the ever-transforming nature of art!

And that's not all. While walking the streets of your city, have you ever spotted a big, striking image painted on a wall? You can find this wall art on houses, offices or any other building (though these are sometimes done without the permission of the wall's owner!). It can be colourful or even black-and-white. This sort of art, for obvious reasons, is called street art. In the five years since 2012, several urban street art projects have come up, and you can see stunning colourful drawings brightening up many city streets.

All these types of contemporary art tend to spark a dialogue that leads to the audience or the onlooker rethinking an idea in a new light. Of course, the forms mentioned above are only the tip of the iceberg of what's possible in the world of art. For in contemporary art, you're only limited by your imagination!

The Money Game

Did you know that a piece of art can sell for lakhs or even crores of rupees? Why do you think people spend such huge sums of money on modern and contemporary art? Well, to understand this, we will have to go back in time.

Before the 1800s or so, the process of selling art was different from what it is now. Earlier, as is explained in this book, the works of art were usually commissioned by a patron—a king, a religious sect, the state or the wealthy class—which meant that art was made to order. And in this case, the patron decided what the subject of the work of art would be, how long it should take to complete and how much an artist should be paid for the piece of art. But as empires rose and fell, artists were left with no patrons. With the coming of the British, and the kingly courts becoming less wealthy and influential, Indian artists started creating works for the new rulers, which were heavily influenced by Western styles of painting. The artists survived on British commissions till the surge of patriotism during India's struggle for independence, when they started creating art to support

Art under the Hammer

Apart from the various art galleries and museums, some national and international auction houses, such as Sotheby's, Christie's, Saffronart and Osian's, have contributed greatly to making the Indian art scene more dynamic. They regularly organize live and/or online auctions wherein artworks of modern and contemporary artists are up for grabs!

the cause of freedom. In independent India, the state took over the role of the traditional patrons and opened art institutions like Lalit Kala Akademi to support and encourage artists.

But before the birth and rise of modern art in India, art that was produced in the country had little demand internationally as Indian art was considered merely decorative. It was only after the arrival of modernism in Indian art that it started getting noticed and appreciated by people across the world, and thus a market for Indian art came into existence. Also, alongside the new international market of the mid-nineties, a local market as well as auction houses emerged, which helped Indian art reach larger audiences right here in India. As Western museums and private collectors began to take notice of unique and valuable pieces of Indian art, the prices of these pieces rose from a few thousand dollars to as high as, in some cases, millions of dollars!

But who decides the price of these works of art, you ask? Well, like the price of most commodities, such as vegetables, fruit, sugar, rice, etc., the price of art also depends on demand and supply. It's simple economics, really! When you have something in abundance, its demand and price are both low. But if something is rare, its demand and price will obviously go up! So if there's great demand for a particular artist's particular artwork, then the price of that piece will be high. Many of the most famous modern Indian artists, like M.F. Husain and S.H. Raza, are sadly no longer with us and won't be creating paintings any more. So this makes their existing works extremely valuable. It's the same thing with artworks from the previous eras. There are only so many paintings from the Mughal times, for instance—so this dramatically affects their pricing.

But what about the artists who are still creating works of art? What drives the prices of their works? Um . . . the same demand and supply! Even if the artist is alive, they can only create a certain number of pieces of art. The demand would still be more than the supply, and thus the prices would remain high. Also, each work of art is unique, and an artist doesn't usually create multiple copies of the same work. Think about it—there is normally only *one original piece* of a particular artwork available! This too tends to be a contributing factor in the high value and prices of artworks. What's more, art dealers, galleries and museums play a huge role in determining which art is good and valuable and which artist should be promoted. This way, they set the base value of any art, which increases further in the future.

In the earlier times, paintings usually incorporated gold and rare materials, like precious and semi-precious stones, to make a statement about the status of the patron kings, and this is what made these paintings valuable. But today, it's the artist's expression, their ideas and concepts that makes their art a treasure. M.F. Husain could have just scribbled a small drawing on a scrap of cloth and it would still cost a million! The prices of modern and contemporary art have moved up in lurches over the last couple of decades, and recently even big corporates are starting to open up their purses to invest in art. This is somewhat like buying a building and waiting for the prices to soar before selling it off. In this case, they buy art in the hope that the market price of the artwork will increase in time and they can later benefit from its sale.

Catch the Real Thing!

There are many galleries in all the major Indian cities, where you can find good collections of contemporary art by famous Indian artists. Among those, four must-sees are **National Gallery of Modern Art (NGMA)**, **Kiran Nadar Museum of Art (KNMA)**, **India Art Fair (IAF)** and **Kochi-Muziris Biennale (KMB)**.

Where: Delhi and Kochi, Kerala

Entry:
- **NGMA:** Rs 20 for Indian nationals; free admission for children below eighteen years of age; Rs 500 for foreign nationals
- **KNMA:** Free entry for all
- **IAF:** Rs 350 for students; Rs 600 for general entry
- **KMB:** Rs 100 for adults; Rs 50 for children up to fifteen years of age

What to see:
- The New Wing at the NGMA houses a variety of stunning contemporary paintings.

A Recap: What's Next?

Today, more than ever, art is about asking questions, debating, engaging in conversations and, of course, setting your own rules. You would already know by now that it's as much or perhaps more about ideas, concepts and feelings as it is about how an artwork looks. Contemporary artists want us to open our eyes and see the world differently through their eyes. They want us to get involved in the art—by observing the small details, exploring the whole art process and the context it is created in, questioning the artwork as well as the realities of the times and, of course, enjoying it. Thanks to the various pioneers of contemporary art, art in India has been able to break free from all constraints of how it should look and what it should say. This has given rise to a new kind of confidence among the young and upcoming artists who are stunning the world with their original approach to art and are busy putting their own twists to art as we speak.

○ The IAF, held every year, and the KMB, held every other year, are art festivals where you can *experience* modern Indian art all around you!

Remember: Do take a look at how the paintings are laid out in the museum or gallery. Have they been hung chronologically or thematically? Or do they focus on the work of one particular artist? Also try to look at the exact name of the painting, the artist's name, when the painting was created, the medium of the painting (such as ink on paper or oil on canvas) and any other such key detail.

Know more at: www.ngmaindia.gov.in; www.knma.in; www.indiaartfair.in; www .kochimuzirisbiennale.org

The Story of Indian Art Continues

How can you capture everything about the world of Indian art in a single book? The answer is simple: you can't. For reasons of pace and space, not all artists and artworks in the history of Indian art have been covered in this book—though an earnest attempt has been made to include those that tell a comprehensive story of Indian art based on the time they are set in.

Even so, if you think that some important artwork has been unfairly left out, that should not hold you back from enjoying it! Go ahead and make notes on it: its features, use of colours and also the idea behind it. Why stop there? Make a whole list of museums and art galleries in your city and get prepped with a detailed map of the floors, a notepad and plenty of curiosity! Or, since this is the twenty-first century, you can even make use of the Internet and visit the websites of these museums, which have well-curated details about their artefacts. And, of course, there are many more art books, in which you can read all about other artists and their works, or learn more about the ones you've already met in these pages. Your art journey's only just begun—turn the page and get exploring!

Acknowledgements

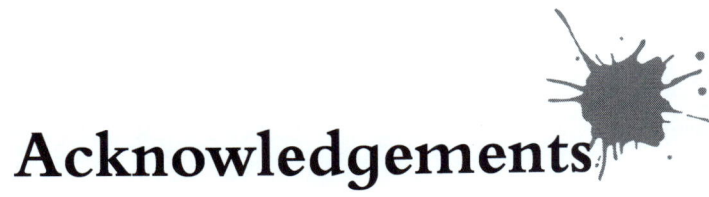

I owe many grateful thanks to . . .

All the artists whose works have stunned me, inspired me and sometimes puzzled me; and to the army of great art historians and writers who did the real work of paving the way for art study—I've only followed their directions.

The National Gallery of Modern Art, Lalit Kala Akademi and Raza Foundation, for very kindly allowing the use of reproductions of their exhibited paintings in this book.

My three fabulous editors, Sohini Mitra, Arpita Nath and Kankana Basu, for their brilliant suggestions, efficiency and editorial finesse that have turned some messy jottings into a book.

My family, for always being so generously supportive of my endeavours.

And, above all, Ona, for training my eyes and infecting me with his passion for art, for serving as a sounding board for my ideas, for always spurring me on, for just being.

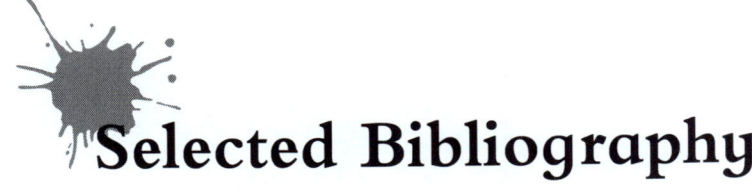

Selected Bibliography

Chaitanya, Krishna. *A History of Indian Painting: The Modern Period*. New Delhi: Abhinav Publications, 1994.

Coomaraswamy, Ananda K. *Introduction to Indian Art*. Delhi: Munshiram Manoharlal, 1969.

Dalmia, Yashodhara, ed. *Contemporary Indian Art: Other Realities*. Mumbai: The Marg Foundation, 2003.

———. *The Making of Modern Indian Art: The Progressives*. New Delhi: Oxford University Press, 2001.

Guha-Thakurta, Tapati. *The Making of 'New' Indian Art: Artists, Aesthetics and Nationalism in Bengal, c. 1850–1920*. Cambridge South-Asian Studies Series. Cambridge: Cambridge University Press, 1992.

Jain, Jyotindra. *Kalighat Paintings: Images from a Changing World*. Ahmedabad: Grantha Corporation, 1999.

Kumar, R. Siva, ed. *The Last Harvest: Paintings of Rabindranath Tagore*. Ahmedabad: Mapin Publishing, 2011.

Mitter, Partha. *Art and Nationalism in Colonial India: 1850–1922, Occidental Orientations*. Cambridge: Cambridge University Press, 1994.

———. *Indian Art*. Oxford History of Art Series. Oxford: Oxford University Press, 2001.

Sister Nivedita. *The Ancient Abbey of Ajanta*. Kolkata: Lalmati, 2009.

Read More in Puffin

Lore of the Land: Storytelling Traditions of India
Nalini Ramachandran

Into the land of stories . . .

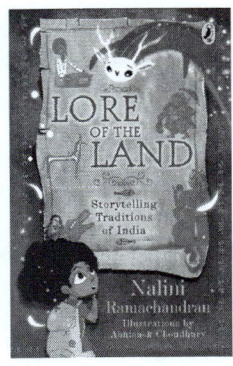

Moody Mohini belongs to a legendary family of storytellers. Telling tall tales is supposed to be in her genes. Except, she doesn't think so—even though her family (as well as just about everyone in Mithika) expects her to be the torchbearer of this rather marvellous tradition.

So, cracking under the pressure of a plot line one day, she runs far away from home, only to be held hostage by a spunky spirit, who traps her in a strange spell and whisks her off on a whirlwind tour of India and its many storytelling traditions. How else can Mohini break the charm (you guessed it!) but by telling a story herself!

Join Mohini as she receives a unique education about the untold ways in which the people of the country weave tales, using everything from stick figures and spectacular sculptures to shadow puppets and flamboyant dance dramas, while discovering the profound powers of that special skill—storytelling.

Read More in Puffin

The Puffin Book of Magical Indian Myths
Anita Nair

A treasure trove of myths from India

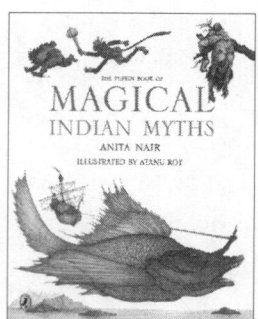

When Surya the sun god got married, his wife could not bear the heat of his rays and ran away. Surya was heartbroken and the world plunged into darkness. A dwarf asked a king for some land, which he measured with three footsteps, and ended up claiming the earth and the sky. Sage Daksha got his daughters married to the moon, but later, in a fit of rage, cursed the moon with consumption, making it wax and wane.

These are some of the fifty myths from India recounted in this fabulously produced book. From wise sages to demonic asuras, beautiful river deities to arrogant kings, wayward gods to brave princes, this collection showcases the most enchanting and magical stories from Indian mythology. With over 100 stunning full-colour illustrations, this book will not only bring alive a fantastic world of gods and demons, it will also be a loved and treasured possession to be enjoyed for many years.

Read More in Puffin

Let's Go Time Travelling!
Life in India through the Ages
Subhadra Sen Gupta

Was King Ashoka fond of chewing paan?
Mulligatawny was a soup, but what was pish-pash?
Did they design jewellery in Harappa?
Who played pachisi, chaupar and lam turki?

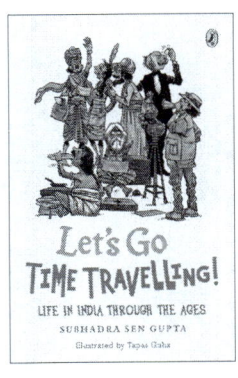

Find the answers to all these weird, impossible questions in this fascinating book about how people lived in the past. Go time travelling through the alleys of history and take a tour through the various ages—from Harappa to the Mauryan, Mughal to the British. Through short snapshots and wacky trivia, this book gives you a glimpse into the vibrant culture of India, as you learn about the life and times of kings, queens, viceroys and even ordinary children!

Spend a day with Urpi as she tries selling pottery in exchange for a few beads at Mohen-jo-daro; step back into King Ashoka's kingdom where Madhura prepares to be a warrior; watch Adil harbor hopes of becoming a khansama in British India.

From food fads to fashion, art and craft to entertainment, this book gives funny, freaky information that no textbook ever will. Peppered with Tapas Guha's crazy cartoons, *Let's Go Time Travelling* makes history fun like never before.